A Democracy Movement Journal: Changchun, China 1989

Jay Lieberman

Table of Contents

Author's Note
March 2014

The following is a revised version of a journal I kept during the 1989 Democracy Movement in China when I was an English teacher at the Jilin University of Technology in Changchun, China. The journal documents the three weeks from the start of the Democracy Movement on our campus to my family's exit from China after June 4th.

I am publishing this account of the Democracy Movement in a city outside of Beijing so readers will better understand the massive size of that movement, the depth of feeling of the participants, and the risks taken by the young people who stood up to the Chinese Communist Party and government.

This journal is a record of the events that occurred in Changchun, not a political analysis of that Movement. In the journal I report what we saw, what we heard, and what we did along with some personal reactions to the events.

When I revised my original journal, I
- Deleted vague and repetitive text
- Reordered events in the daily entries so they were in time order
- Added footnotes for explanatory materials
- Added missing names of Party leaders
- Added translations of significant phrases in the 1989 speeches of Party leaders
- Added the transcriptions done by my wife Sally Lieberman of the character posters and signs that she saw in Changchun during that period. Sally, a PhD student in Chinese

Literature in 1989, and several volunteers translated those transcriptions. Missing or illegible characters are represented by a question mark in brackets [?].

- Added photographs taken by Sally or me.
- Did everything I could to make everyone in the book other than my family members unidentifiable
- Did not update the names of schools and streets in Changchun that have changed since 1989 (e.g., Jilin Tech is now part of Jilin University).

Prologue

They're going to get shot.

That's what I was thinking as I watched two dozen university students march up a street in Changchun, China on June 5, 1989. They marched in four rows with their arms intertwined, led by three pairs of students carrying large funeral wreaths.

The students were marching to protest the murder the day before of hundreds, possibly thousands, of students and residents in Beijing by Chinese army troops. The students marched to mourn for the dead but also to spread the message among the people of Changchun that the Chinese government's reports on the situation were lies.

Marching up that street was a very dangerous thing to do. The provincial government had declared martial law in Changchun that morning and any gathering of more than three people was banned. The provincial government had allowed Democracy Movement rallies and demonstrations during May, but there were rumors that Chinese army troops were now stationed outside the city, ready to use force against protesters.

Were there troops waiting a few blocks away on People's Circle with orders to shoot these kids? Were there police waiting on a side street, ready to push the students onto buses that would take them to a place where confessions would be coerced and prison sentences decreed?

My eyes filled with tears as I watched the marchers from the safety of a University car. Would I be brave

7

enough to march if I didn't know what was waiting
farther up the road?

Introduction: Nine Quiet Months in China, and Then....

When the Democracy Movement began in Spring 1989, my family had been living for nine months in Changchun, the capital of Jilin province, located about 750 miles northeast of Beijing. My wife, Sally, and I were language teachers at the Jilin University of Technology, giving mostly-bored undergraduates some exposure to native English speakers to help them pass their national English exam. Seven-year-old Michael was in first grade at Jilin Tech's primary school and four-year-old Hannah was a student in Jilin Tech's kindergarten. We lived in a large apartment in an old campus building inside a fenced foreigners compound that also contained a foreign students dorm.

During the nine months before the Democracy Movement, our family had a regular routine of teaching, shopping, schoolwork, and study that kept us busy from 6 a.m. until 9 or 10 p.m. On weekends we had time to go to a restaurant for a meal or take a family excursion on our bikes, but Changchun had few interesting places to visit or exciting events to attend. Life there was dull, predictable, and safe.

In mid-April the Democracy Movement started in Beijing during the official mourning period for Hu Yaobang, a purged Communist Party leader respected by Chinese liberals and intellectuals. On Tiananmen Square, the official center of national mourning, students began to publicly raise the demands for change they had been formulating on their Beijing campuses for the last year. They demanded action against government corruption and changes to China's ongoing economic reforms,

9

reforms that are making a handful of people rich and impoverishing millions.

I wasn't aware that the student movement had reached Changchun until May 4th, when Sally and I watched large groups of students from other Changchun campuses march in support of the Beijing students' demands.

Jilin Tech students did not participate in the May 4th rallies. They spent the morning in classes and the afternoon in a mandatory assembly that was set up, I presumed, to keep them away from the demonstrations. I found out later that the Jilin Tech administration had warned our students that they could be dismissed from the university if they got involved in the new movement. Dismissal would be a serious black mark on their personal record that could be used against them for the rest of their lives.

After May 4th, I didn't go to any Changchun demonstrations or pay much attention to news reports about the growing Democracy Movement in Beijing. I was concentrating on finishing up the school year and preparing to leave in early June for a week in Beijing and then a flight back to Minnesota. I didn't expect anything dramatic to happen on our campus before the end of the school year.

I was wrong.

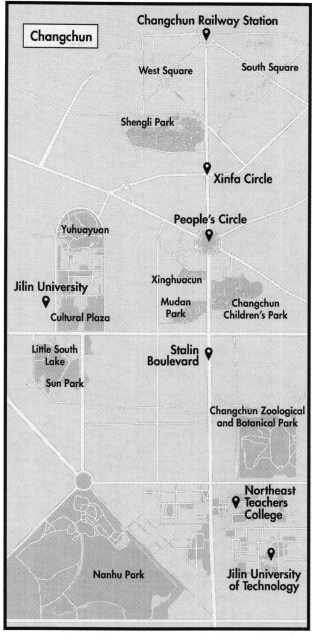

Illustration: Amy C. Smith 2015

Democracy Movement Journal

5/16 Tuesday

Today, the student movement came to our campus.

Classes were cancelled today because it was Sports Day, the annual intramural competition between the Jilin Tech departments. The foreign teachers were all invited to watch, so about noon we walked from our apartment to the school's athletic field. When we arrived our family was seated on the official reviewing stand, next to some fellow teachers and behind a row of senior professors and staffers from the Waiban[1].

---

[1] Short for "Waishi banchu," translated as "Foreign Affairs Office."

Sports Day began with a parade around the track. The flag contingent came first, followed by the students marching behind their department banners. The students, decked out in their tracksuits, looked much happier than they did when they were sitting in English class.

As soon as the parade ended, the competition began. Over the next few hours we watched running races, field events like the long jump, martial arts competitions, and even a tug of war. We cheered for all the students and had no idea which department was in the lead.

Midafternoon, someone ran up to the reviewing stand and reported to the faculty members that a large group of students from Jilin University, the big provincial liberal arts school across town, was marching toward the field. When the news reached our row on the reviewing stand I was surprised and very excited. The Democracy Movement was coming to us!

A minute later we saw the first row of marchers come level with the field's west gate. I grabbed Hannah's and Mike's hands and headed for the edge of the platform. One of the Waiban staff came over and urged us to stay on the platform where it would be safer, but I was determined to see the Jilin University march up close. I told him we would be careful and we continued off the platform.

We jumped to the ground and ran a few yards to the chain link fence that separated the field from the street. On the other side of the fence, row after row of Jilin University students marched by us, chanting jubilantly and pumping their fists. I only understood one of the chants-- "Gongda, bu hai pa" (Tech students, don't be afraid!). The Jilin Tech students standing around me on our side of the fence watched silently.

A roar went up at the east end of the field. I turned that way and saw the Jilin University students coming in through the east gate and onto the track. Our students surged to the east side of the field and joined the Jilin University march, and that combined mass of cheering and chanting people slowly moved around the running track. I ran back to the platform with the kids to get some pictures.

The march went halfway around the track and then out the west gate. I think a large number of Sports Day participants left with the Jilin University students.

As the marchers moved down the street and away from the field, a buzz of excited voices came from the remaining Jilin Tech students. The Sports Day announcer called for the sports events to begin again but we headed home.

∞∞∞∞∞∞∞∞∞

A few hours later, as we were finishing our dinner, we heard a lot of noise coming from the street that runs behind our apartment building, an old two-story building located at the edge of the Jilin Tech foreigner's compound. When we ran upstairs and out onto our rear balcony we saw several hundred enthusiastic students marching down the street behind a big banner. They waved to us as they went past.

We wanted to find out what was going on so we hurried out of our apartment building, walked through the foreigners' compound gate, and merged into the stream of chanting students. We walked with them to the commons area in the middle of the Automobile Department dorms where a large crowd was already gathered.

Some students we knew told us that the Jilin Tech Student Council agreed to sponsor a march tonight to support the Beijing students. The students said in the past month the Student Council had refused to sponsor activities in support of the Beijing students but today the Jilin Tech student activists wouldn't take no for an answer. Jilin Tech students will meet students from Jilin University and other schools at the Changchun newspaper office and together they'll demand that the newspaper provide more balanced coverage of the Beijing student movement.[2]

As we stood and talked, the Student Council members were lining up students behind Jilin Tech department banners. In a little while, the first department in line moved forward, headed toward the school's main gate at Stalin Boulevard.[3]

At that point Sally and I agreed that I would take the bike and go with the students tonight while Sally stayed with the kids. She will go with the next march while I watch the kids.

---

[2] By this date, the student movement that began on the Beijing university campuses had grown in a broader movement that was centered on Tianmen Square in Central Beijing.

[3] Stalin Boulevard was named in acknowledgement of the Russian liberation of Changchun from a brutal WWII Japanese occupation. It was later renamed to People's Boulevard.

When the lead department banner reached the Jilin Tech Main Gate, the Student Council members stopped the march and reorganized the students into narrower rows of five across. When the council members finished tidying the lines, the march moved through the gate and started north on Stalin.

Stalin Boulevard is one of the main north/south streets in Changchun. The avenue has four car lanes with a very wide bicycle/animal cart lane on each side, separated from the car lanes by a wide divider. The students were marching in the bicycle lane and I was walking my bike alongside them, more an observer than a participant.

As we walked the mile or so north to Peoples Circle, groups of students from the small schools and institutes that line Stalin Boulevard joined the march and it swelled to three or four thousand people. Soon the march filled the bicycle lane while more people walked alongside on the sidewalk or pushed their bikes in one of the main traffic lanes (which resulted in a lot of honking by angry drivers).

The few policemen that I saw on Stalin were just observing the march, not obstructing or challenging it. The marchers were extremely friendly with the police.

The Jilin Tech students were happy and excited-- smiling and waving to the people we passed and chanting loudly. Students who would never say a word during English class left their place in the march and walked with me for a few minutes, asking me how I liked the march and if I supported the Beijing students.

The answer to the first question was easy--I told them I was really enjoying the march--but the second question was more difficult to answer. First, I really didn't know enough about the Beijing students' demands to have an educated opinion about them. Second, I was concerned that if I endorsed the student's demands, the Waiban would be angry that an American teacher was telling students that it was right to rebel against the government. I gave the safe answer to the second question, saying I needed to learn more about the students' demands before I could comment on them.

I asked students who walked with me to translate the marcher's chants into English. They reported that the chants denounced government corruption and demanded that the government take action on economic problems like inflation and social problems like the declining quality of education across China. The chants also denounced the poor quality of life of students and intellectuals.

As we neared People's Circle some of the marchers began to sing the Internationale, the anthem of the international Communist movement. These students had sung the Internationale hundreds or even thousands of times in praise of the Chinese Communist Party, but now it was being sung to protest the way the Communist Party ran the state. The students looked a bit embarrassed or confused when the song started, but eventually they overcame their reluctance and, by the final chorus, everyone had joined in and was singing exuberantly.

When the march reached Peoples Circle, I saw a number of police stationed at the circle's intersections and I started worrying. Would the police want to question me since I was a foreigner at a student protest? I wouldn't be able to clearly identify myself or explain why I was there because my spoken Chinese is very limited and I didn't have my passport, my resident foreigner card, or my Jilin Tech employment card with me. My fear of an encounter with the police was stronger than my curiosity about the rally, so I decided to go back home.

During my ride home, Stalin Boulevard was deserted except for a few small groups of people talking quietly on street corners. This was the first time all year I had been alone in the city at night so I was a bit nervous but I was still enjoying the buzz from the excitement of the march. Interesting times are ahead.

5/17 Wednesday

This morning some students told me that after I left the circle, the Jilin Tech students rallied at the newspaper office, marched to the railway station at the north end of downtown, and then marched back to campus. They said they cheered, chanted, and banged on pots in the dorm areas until very late (very late may have been the regular lights out at 11 p.m.). I didn't hear any banging late last night but I am a pretty sound sleeper.

They also said that there is going to be another Student Council-sanctioned march this afternoon. Just two days ago no one on this campus talked openly about the Beijing students but now everyone is marching to support them! Obviously there was a lot of conversation about the Beijing students' demands that my students didn't share with me.

∞∞∞∞∞∞∞∞∞∞

After lunch we could see students gathering in the Auto dorm commons and on the street a few blocks from our apartment. We walked up to the group gathering on the street and watched them line up behind several banners, probably a mix of department banners and banners with student movement slogans.

When they were lined up, the students began marching toward the school's main gate. It was

Sally's turn to go with the marchers so she followed them out toward Stalin Boulevard.

The students marched north on Stalin Boulevard for a while, then turned west and marched to the Jilin University campus where their Sports Day was going on. Our students marched onto the athletic field like the Jilin University students marched onto our field, but their Sports Day announcer welcomed the marchers and called out the names of the Jilin Tech departments as the banners came around the track!

The marchers left the Jilin University campus and went back to Stalin Boulevard, then headed north to the Jilin provincial government building on Xinfa Circle. The provincial government headquarters, a new eight-story building, is located between two major downtown shopping areas that include Department stores #5 and #2. Demonstrations in this area are seen by thousands of shoppers.

The Jilin Tech march, maybe 5000 strong at this point, got to the provincial government building and stopped. After a rally and some discussion, the march returned to campus.

Later, we were told that when the march reached the provincial government building, the Jilin Tech Student Council leaders ordered our students to turn back. Some of the students refused and marched another half mile to join a protest of the train station's refusal to sell tickets to Beijing to students.

Sally saw new posters with messages supporting the Beijing students on blank walls downtown and on our campus.

∞∞∞∞∞∞∞∞∞∞

Students from Changchun's universities and institutes are going to show support for the Beijing students by sending ten to fifty representatives from each school to the center of the student movement on Tiananmen Square in Beijing. Students all over the city are collecting money to help pay for the representatives' train tickets and other expenses.

Students on our campus are having a spirited debate about who their student representatives should be. The Jilin Tech administration wants the student council members to be the school's representatives but many of our students want to choose their representatives democratically like other Changchun schools have done.

Changchun students are also talking about going on strike in support of ongoing strikes by students at the Beijing universities. The students at all the Changchun schools are going to take strike votes soon.

The Jilin Tech student strike meeting is tonight. The students I've talked to strongly support the Beijing students' demands but I don't know if they will vote for a strike. These students have worked very hard to earn their place in a university and going on strike could put their university education and possibly their careers in jeopardy.

∞∞∞∞∞∞∞∞

I think I now have a pretty good understanding of the two main points being raised by the student movement. First, the students are angry about the inequities caused by the current economic reforms, reforms that were designed by Deng Xiaoping and are now directed by Zhao Ziyang. [4] The students say

---

[4] Deng, a Party activist since the 1949 Chinese revolution, twice survived being purged from the Communist Party for his strong support of economic liberalization. After Mao's death, his theory of a "socialist market economy" became the core philosophy driving

those reforms have allowed a small group of people--speculators and well connected entrepreneurs--to get rich while the salaries of professional people like engineers, professors, and doctors stagnate.

The economic reforms are also causing severe problems for people in the countryside. The students say the government has slashed support for agriculture, causing a collapse in the farm economy that is forcing millions of rural people to migrate to distant cities to find work.

Second, the Beijing students attack a growing culture of corruption in the Party and government that helps well-connected people and relatives of the Party leaders get rich through guandao--institutional bribery and graft. The students say Deng Xiaoping's son Deng Pufong, and Zhao Ziyang's son Zhao Erjun (who everyone says is making a fortune selling imported TVs) are examples of insiders getting rich because of their connections.

Although I don't think it's a major issue for the student movement, our students are also pretty fed up with their educational and living conditions. The main classroom building we teach in has dirty walls,

---

China's growth into a global economic power. In 1989 his only official post was Chairman of the Central Military Commission but he was considered by most to be the "paramount leader" of China. Zhao Ziyang was General Secretary of the Communist Party in 1989. In the period after the 1960s Cultural Revolution he established market-oriented reforms called the "Sichuan Experience" that Deng cited as a model for all of China. Zhao believed that democratization had to be linked to economic progress in order for his reforms to succeed and he worked on democratic reforms with Hu Yaobang until Hu was forced to retire and Zhao was given his leadership positions.

broken windows, and scary wiring that requires touching two live wires together to turn on the lights. During the winter, the students sit for eight hours a day in classrooms that are so cold they have to wear their down coats to stay warm.[5] They also have to use cloth covers to protect their coat sleeves and books from the coal soot that always finds its way onto their desks.

Student living conditions are cramped. The dorm rooms for undergraduates contain eight beds (four bunk beds) and two closets crowded into a room with concrete walls and floors. There are only four students in a graduate student dorm room and each student has a desk, but it's still cramped. There are large communal bathrooms in every dorm, but the showers, which students have to pay for, are in a different building. The distribution point for boiled water is also in a separate building that students trudge to with their thermoses once or twice a day.[6]

The students are also pretty unhappy with the quantity and quality of food in their cafeteria. I found out that the cafeteria doesn't make enough food for each meal to feed all the students, so students who arrive last at meal times find the cafeteria line closed. If they're too late to get cafeteria food, the students have to buy food at a restaurant or a store, an extra expense that many of them can't afford. Apparently tempers run so high in the race for food that last year a fight over butting in the cafeteria line led to an accidental death and a series of student protests.

---

[5] Changchun, located 750 km northeast of Beijing, had long, cold winters.
[6] All drinking water in China must be boiled.

25

The cafeteria meals usually consist of a large portion of rice and a small portion of meat and vegetables. While there are some students who say the food is okay, most of them, particularly the students from southern China, complain about the lack of variety of dishes, the taste of the food, and the size of the portions. They don't feel any better when I tell them that that we pay a lot more for the food at the foreigners' cafeteria but the quality of the food isn't much better than theirs.

∞∞∞∞∞∞∞∞

Every day I piece together news from a variety of sources to get a picture of what's going on inside and outside of China.

We rely on the students and teachers we know to keep us informed about what's going on in Changchun and on our campus and to get us news from their friends and family in Beijing. A lot of the stories we hear from them are probably rumors but they are our only source for local information.

We get a lot of China and international news from shortwave radio broadcasts. I listen to VOA (Voice of America) news every morning, I usually listen to the BBC news in the afternoon, and I occasionally hear a Radio Japan broadcast in English in the evenings. More shortwave broadcasts in English are probably available but I often have problems tuning in less powerful broadcasts on the old, somewhat unreliable shortwave receiver that came with our apartment.

We also get some information from China's national TV news which is on every night at 7 p.m. on CCTV1, one of the two government-controlled TV channels-- the only TV channels we can get in Changchun. The news broadcast (in Chinese, of course) usually contains reports on campaigns against crime (e.g., the arrest of a scrap metal theft ring), coverage of foreign dignitary visits, video from prospering factories and farms, and some world news. As far as we can tell, the CCTV national news is not reporting on the Beijing demonstrations.

This spring, CCTV introduced a news broadcast in English at 10 p.m. (late-night TV in China!) that mainly presents world news. This news broadcast has reported on the student movement.

Our last news source is the Christian Science Monitor print edition that we receive by airmail a week after it's published. The news may be stale but the paper usually contains interesting analyses of world events.

∞∞∞∞∞∞∞∞

Sally began recording the chants she heard at rallies and the contents of banners and wall posters.

Banner Slogans and Chants, 5/17 – 5/19

走向何方中国？	Where is China heading?
妈妈，我们为您奋起	Mother, we are fighting for you
向绝食同学敬礼！	We salute our fasting classmates!
爱国无罪	Patriotism is not a crime

跟着良心走	Follow your conscience
伟大学生运动万岁！	Long live the great student movement!
惩［官[7]］倒！反腐败！	Punish corrupt officials! Oppose corruption!
要求政府正上对话	We demand a formal dialogue with the government
打倒［官］	Overturn corrupt officials
为什么不敢说真话？	Why are you afraid to tell the truth?
麻木者，良心何在？	Apathetic people, where is your conscience?
庸才，下台！	Mediocre people, step down!
沉默就是死	Silence is death
提高知识分子经济地位	Improve the economic status of intellectuals

[7] In several of the slogans, the character guan is upside down. This is a visual pun; the word for official corruption is guandao; the "dao" literally means upside down, and has been omitted because the upside-down "guan" (official) implies the same thing.

"老的不推出来，新的进不去！"——邓小平

"If you don't push out the old, the new can't get in!" Deng Xiaoping

Jilin Tech Democracy Wall Posters, 5/17 -5/19

成立学生自治会

Form an independent student organization.

机会者下台!

Opportunists step down!

报露：昨天我们在学生会的"带领"之下声势浩大地的举行了"春游，"并争取到十个所去京名领。然而学生会又声称去京学生全是自费。校方不予[   ]支持。那么我要问：昨天我们[?]捐的钱在哪里？这钱不用于学生请愿上京，难道我们又要被"学生倒"倒吗？

Yesterday under the "leadership" of the Student

Council we had a huge "spring outing" and we won ten places for people to go to Beijing. [8] However, the Student Council now says the travel expense is the responsibility of the individuals who are traveling so there's no financial support from the school. We have to ask: where is the money we donated yesterday? If that money is not used for the students going to Beijing, are we going to be ripped off by "corrupt student officials"?

总理总理总不理	Premier, Premier, he doesn't care
何时对话何时复课	We won't go back to classes until we have a dialogue

[8] Spring Outing refers to the officially approved demonstration on the evening of the 16th.

5/18 Thursday

This morning, VOA reported that over a million people marched through the streets of Beijing to Tiananmen Square in support of students there in the fifth day of a hunger strike. There were also demonstrations in twenty of China's twenty-six provincial capitals. This includes the demonstrations yesterday in Changchun, which is the capital of Jilin Province.

I wasn't scheduled to teach this morning, but I walked to Classroom Building #1 to see if the students were on strike. As I approached, I saw a lot of students leaving the building even though there was still one hour left in the class period. When I went inside I saw students milling around in the hall and several empty classrooms.

Later Sally told me that her students came to class but they didn't look like they wanted to stay. She said they did settle down and pay attention to the lesson she taught, even ignoring a person who walked down the hall banging on a pot and calling for students to strike.

When I left the classroom building I saw a small group of students reading large handwritten posters on a wall across the street from the building. These "big character" posters are the way people in China who have no access to newspapers or even copy machines have spread information during all of

China's modern political upheavals. While I was crossing the street to take a look, a new poster went up and the students cheered.

One of the students greeted me as I approached the wall and explained that most of the posters criticized the Jilin Tech student council leaders for not organizing enough demonstrations to support the Beijing University students. The posters called for Jilin Tech students to overthrow their student council leaders or at least push them into more action.

Someone told me that today the Jilin Tech administration announced that it's okay for students to demonstrate in support of the Beijing students but they absolutely cannot go on strike—the same policy the Jilin provincial government announced recently. Would the Jilin Tech administration really punish large numbers of students if they went on strike? Will our students go on strike knowing they might be punished?

∞∞∞∞∞∞∞∞∞

I went back to the apartment, turned on the TV and was surprised to see a live CCTV broadcast of several Central Committee leaders visiting a Beijing hospital. As the cameras followed the Party leaders through the building, we could see young people lying on cots in the hallway and on beds in crowded rooms. These must be the student hunger strikers who are too sick to stay on Tiananmen.

The cameras followed Li Peng as he went into one of

the rooms and walked to a student's bedside. [9] Li told the student to bring his grievances to the government but not in this way and to take care of his health.

The students in the room were respectful but they also made it clear that they were firm in their beliefs. One student struggled up onto his elbow to tell several of China's leaders that the country had four problems—a huge population, unfair economic reforms, corruption, and the poor treatment of intellectuals. Li responded that these were hard problems to solve but if China was to be saved the leaders must listen to the people right now. The broadcast ended after a few more exchanges between Li and the students in that room.

I think the leaders went to the hospital to give the hunger strikers a paternalistic pat on the head but not to start a true dialogue. If the leaders wanted a dialogue, wouldn't they talk with the student leaders who are at the center of the protest on Tiananmen Square?

∞∞∞∞∞∞∞∞∞∞

I don't think the demands for change coming from all across China will be satisfied by small adjustments to the economic reforms or a new government campaign against corruption. People who support the student movement don't believe that the Communist Party

---

[9] Li Peng was Premier of the State Council in 1989 and one of Zhao Ziyang's major critics, arguing that Zhao's democratic reforms would lead to instability that would undermine the authority of the Communist Party. In 1988, he had joined a leadership group that called for greater centralization of the economy and stricter prohibitions against Zhao's approach.

and the government it controls are acting in the best interests of all the Chinese people. Now that Hu Yaobang is dead, no one trusts the current leaders; they say Deng is too old, Li Peng is just following Deng's orders, and Zhao is the architect of the inequities that the students are protesting.

∞∞∞∞∞∞∞∞∞

Jilin Tech sent ten representatives to Beijing on the 17th after the Jilin Tech student rally. Many Jilin Tech students didn't think those representatives, all student council members, spoke out strongly enough in support of the Beijing student demands so ten additional representatives were elected and sent to Beijing soon after. I think more students may have gone on their own.

Today I was told that both our school and Northeast Teachers University, which borders the Jilin Tech campus on the north, are on strike. That means more students will go to Beijing since they won't be going to classes.

What are all these students doing in Beijing? The city must be a madhouse with tens of thousands of students descending on it from all over the country.

∞∞∞∞∞∞∞∞∞

After a long year of tedious routine, I now have the feeling that something interesting could happen any minute. Right now, the Northeast Teachers students living at a dorm not far from our apartment are protesting the bad food in their cafeteria by throwing bottles, cans, and even burning paper out of their windows. [10]

∞∞∞∞∞∞∞∞

The Waiban called us today to tell us their official position on how foreign teachers, as guests of the Chinese government, should relate to the Democracy Movement. Mainly they told us to stay away from the demonstrations because they could turn violent. Sally told them that we were aware of the possible dangers, that we would be very careful, and that we had no intention of seeking trouble.

∞∞∞∞∞∞∞∞

Tonight, CCTV news reported on a meeting between Li Peng and a few of the Beijing student leaders. I think the meeting was meant as a partial recognition of the movement since it was held in a very ornate meeting room where Chinese leaders often greet foreign leaders. Although we couldn't understand a lot of what was being said, it was clear from Li's body language and the tone of his voice that this was not an equal dialogue. He warned the students that they were creating chaos in Beijing and that couldn't be tolerated.

For a long time after the news, the street behind our apartment was busy with students marching past or roaring by on flatbed trucks.

---

[10] Deng's personal name, Xiaoping is a homonym in Chinese for "small bottle."

Posters on Classroom Buildings and Democracy Wall, 5/18

工大同胞：

工大同胞们， 我们都有一服爱国热情，但却缺少组织，而学生会却并不能代表我们。我们现在急需一个自治组织团结广大同学联和各高校，进行有组织彻广真正的声援活动！行动起来吧。建立我们自己的组织！

Gongda Compatriots: We all are strongly patriotic but we lack organization and the student council cannot represent us. We're in urgent need of a self-governing organization that can broadly unite the classmates in all the universities and then carry out well-organized, broad and genuine support activities. Let's take action and establish our own organization!

中国的繁荣之梦没有经济上成功。无异于一枕黄粱。腐败的政治制度却抑制了它的发展。唯一的出路便是改良政治和政党员，发展教育，提高全民素质。

China's dream of prosperity has not succeeded in the economic realm. It's tantamount to a pipedream. The corrupt political system is holding back the development of China. The only way out is to reform politics and government and Party personnel, develop education, and improve the character of the whole people.

5/19 Friday

Jilin Tech students met on campus until 3 a.m. this morning, planning a rally for today and discussing how to strengthen their strike. Student representatives also went to a citywide meeting to discuss how to build support in Changchun for the Beijing students. Some of the Jilin Tech representatives at that meeting stayed on Xinfa Circle to join the hunger strike.

While I know students are joining the hunger strike to show the depth of their support for the Beijing students, I'm worried that the government will refuse to discuss the students' demands and these idealistic young people will be permanently injured or even die from fasting. Why won't the government at least talk to the students and prevent that from happening?!

This morning no students came to my scheduled conversation class and strike slogans were written on the chalkboard. I walked to the nearby English teachers' lounge where my peers told me that all the classrooms in the building are empty.

(On the blackboard) All people with conscience rise and strike! Protest! Strike!; Fellow classmates with conscience will not go to class!; Strike!

While I was talking with them about the strike, the lead instructor for the freshman conversation class came into the room. That person told us that we must always report to our scheduled classes on time and we must teach our lesson if there are <u>any</u> students in the classroom, but we can leave if there are no students in the room. The lead instructor said that if we don't follow those rules, our teaching contracts will be ended. After the lead instructor left, the other teachers told me they would follow those rules so they can keep their jobs.

When I got back to our apartment, I turned on the TV and was amazed to see live coverage (I think) of Li Peng and Zhao Ziyang on Tiananmen Square. The camera followed the leaders as they walked to one of the buses that the hunger strikers are using for shelter. The camera was right behind Zhao as he entered the bus and used a small megaphone to talk to the students.

Just like in the hospital, the students were respectful and the leader was patronizing. He said "We can't solve the problem by having a six-day hunger strike, screaming, and shouting," "You are still young, take care of your health, you're only eighteen or nineteen, don't sacrifice your lives...I think your intentions are good," and "We can't let the situation go on like this...It's getting bigger every day." The broadcast ended a few minutes later.

After the TV broadcast, I decided to ride downtown to see if anything interesting was happening there.

Everything seemed normal on the Jilin Tech campus, but four or five blocks north on Stalin I saw a standoff in front of a small Provincial office building. A small group of students were standing face to face with an equal number of police who were guarding the building. More police were lined up behind the students to prevent anyone else from joining them. I watched for about five minutes and decided this was a stalemate since the students were probably satisfied that they were making their opinions heard and the police were satisfied the students weren't trying to get closer to the building. I decided to move on.

When I got closer to downtown, I approached the back of a very large march that filled the northbound traffic and bike lanes. I decided to ride around that march so I could see what was going on further up Stalin. I crossed Stalin and rode north on the sidewalk up to People's Circle.

There was no protest activity on People's Circle so I continued north through the heart of downtown to

Xinfa Circle. Five city buses, covered with banners like the Tiananmen buses I just saw on CCTV, were parked in a rough circle in front of the Jilin provincial government building. Protestors were milling around inside the circle of buses while some Changchun residents milled around outside the circle, reading the banners and talking in small groups.

I saw young people sitting quietly inside the buses, watching the activity around them. I assumed they were hunger strikers since they wore headbands like the ones the Beijing hungers strikers are wearing.

Hunger Striker bus on Xinfa Circle, provincial government headquarters in the background.

A Jilin Tech student approached me and asked if I had seen the TV broadcast of the Party leaders' visit to Tiananmen. I said I had. He told me that his classmates were very mad about Zhao Ziyang's statements. He said Changchun students were more determined than ever to continue the hunger strike and protests until the government meets the students' demands.

After I was there for about thirty minutes I began to feel like I was being watched, particularly when I pulled my camera out of my backpack. Perhaps it was just people who are unfamiliar with foreigners watching me—there aren't many foreigners in Changchun—but I'm sure there were also plainclothes police and security personnel in this area. I decided to try to be more discreet when I used my camera.

While I was inside the circle of buses, the crowd outside the circle had doubled or tripled. I decided it might be safest if I went back to our campus, so I moved out to the edge of the crowd. From there I could see small student marches converging on Xinfa Circle from all directions.

I started riding south on Stalin and had just reached People's Circle when I got stuck in a traffic jam caused by a march headed away from downtown. I stopped and waited for that group to move around the circle and down Stalin, but when I started south again I saw a huge march headed north toward me, the largest I had seen so far. I decided to find a spot on the circle where I could watch this march go by.

The march was led by a pickup truck from the Jilin Arts Academy. There was a big painting of Zhou Enlai above the cab of the truck and white flowers and black ribbons were draped around the truck bed.[11] Four or five musicians sitting in the back alternated between playing a funeral dirge and the Chinese national anthem.

By displaying a picture of Zhou, the students were, I think, praising a leader who was always said to be principally concerned with the people's welfare, and

---

[11] Zhou Enlai was a widely respected leader from the early days of the Communist Party, serving as Premier of China from 1949 until his death in 1976. He was China's leading diplomat and was also known for protecting people from the excesses of the Cultural Revolution. After his death the massive public outpouring of grief in Beijing turned to anger towards the Gang of Four, leading to the Tiananmen Incident.

condemning the current leaders who only want money and power for themselves.

I stood on that corner for an hour as I think between 50-100,000 people marched by me. I couldn't tell which schools the students were from but it must have included students from all the Changchun schools participating in the movement.

A group of teachers in the march called out to me in English to join them and one student came over to tell me that students at his school were very mad about Zhao Ziyang's words at Tiananmen that morning. He said the students he knew all thought the government should immediately start an equal dialogue with the students.

Police in their regular uniforms (not riot gear) were stationed at intervals around the circle, watching but not interfering with the march. I thought I was inconspicuous in this mass of people, but I saw a uniformed policeman directly across the street from me start to watch me when I pulled out my camera and took pictures of the truck leading the march. He watched me until I put my camera in my backpack.

I returned home after the march passed by me.

Sally went downtown in the afternoon. She said the buses were still parked on Xinfa and barricades now stopped traffic from going onto the Circle. Students were gathered inside the barricades and a large crowd, probably in the thousands, watched from outside the circle.

Chants and Posters at the Provincial Government Building Sit-in, 5/19

总理总理总不理	Prime Minister, Prime Minister, he doesn't care (Alternative translation: Prime Minister, Prime Minister, Supremely Unconcerned)
何时对话何时复课	We won't go back to class until we have a dialogue.

Sally said she saw a group of students from Harbin (a city several hundred miles north of Changchun) marching around the circle, a group of striking Changchun middle school students marching on another street, and truckloads of unidentifiable students driving around downtown. The police were out in large numbers, but they just watched all the activity.

∞∞∞∞∞∞∞∞∞

The 7 p.m. CCTV news replayed the video of Zhao Ziyang's remarks at Tiananmen and praised the leaders' kind attitude toward the students. The CCTV news in English at 10:15 showed the same highlights as the 7 p.m. news—a disappointment since the English language news broadcast had seemed more sympathetic to the students over the past few weeks.

Near the end of the news in English, a news bulletin

began running across the bottom of the screen--the hunger strike ended at 9 p.m. tonight! I'm glad the hunger strike ended since we don't want these kids to ruin their health, but I'd like to know why it ended. Did the government agree to discuss the student demands?

5/20 Saturday

At 6:00 a.m. the campus loudspeakers started blaring a speech instead of the usual aerobics music. A male speaker was making forceful statements that were responded to with thunderous applause by a large, unseen audience. Looking out the window, I saw a deserted campus. There was no indication that the speech had something to do with a student victory.

The VOA morning broadcast explained what was going on. The speech we heard being repeated over and over on the loudspeakers was Li Peng's announcement that the Party and the government had decided to use People's Liberation Army [PLA] troops to "stabilize" the situation in Beijing and bring the country back into order. As part of this stabilization, the government cut the satellite uplinks and international phone lines that connect China to the world.

VOA reported that people in Beijing are erecting barricades to stop troops from advancing through the city to Tiananmen and student contingents are marching to the edges of the city to try to nonviolently block the progress of troops and to explain their demands to the soldiers.

From our apartment I watched somber-looking students walk by on the way to the cafeteria. Many were walking with their heads down, small portable radios pressed to their ears, probably listening to a rebroadcast of Li Peng's speech.

When I walked out onto campus, I saw that last night someone had torn down all the posters that students had put up in the last few days. A few new posters that reflected the students' anger at Li's speech were being put up as I watched.

Posters on Campus, 5/20

砍头不要紧，	只要主义真!	It's okay to get your head cut off if what you believe is true.
我们的祖国，我们的人民，被强奸了!		Our country, our people, were raped!
是党指挥枪，	还是枪指挥党?	Does the Party command the gun or does the gun command the Party?

This morning VOA also reported that George Bush made a statement supporting the students' fight for "freedom and free enterprise" in the Communist world. He also stated that the current struggle in China showed how socialism had failed.

Those remarks are just stupid, particularly because they're coming from a former US Ambassador to China who should understand that statements like that could be used against the student movement. Bush's statement plays right into the hands of the Communist Party leaders who say the students are anti-socialist and are being manipulated by outsiders and troublemakers.

First of all, freedom, a vague concept that I'm sure George Bush couldn't define, doesn't come up much in the discussions here. Yes, the students want freedom of speech, but more importantly they want a government that listens to the people when they speak and responds to their grievances by resolving the people's problems.

Second, the Beijing students are not demanding free enterprise in China. In fact, our students abhor the growing inequalities that the "free market" is creating in China. The students often talk about how unfair it is that some people are building huge businesses and becoming multi-millionaires while millions of people in the undeveloped regions of the country are being driven into poverty.

It's clear to me that Bush and his people have no understanding of the sentiment behind this student movement.

After listening to the news, I went to my scheduled class in Classroom Building #1. There were a lot of students in my class today but they were somber and not really interested in what I was teaching. One student told me that some of the missing students were at protests elsewhere in Changchun.

After class I talked with one of the Chinese English teachers. That teacher thinks the troops will advance to Tiananmen and disperse the students but this summer, when the students go back to their hometowns, the students and their peers will plan future protests and the movement will grow.

ooooooooooo

What's going on in Beijing right now? We can't get any news from CCTV, which is only broadcasting Li Peng's martial law speech over and over. The VOA and BBC shortwave broadcasts say people in Beijing are nonviolently resisting the army's advance in some parts of the city and fighting police in other areas, but I don't know if they are broadcasting rumors or if their reporters are observing all this activity.

I was told that plain-clothes police are ripping down posters on campus as soon as they are put up. I think the students are getting shyer about visiting to tell us the news because of the increased police presence.

In the evening we took a walk around campus. We saw a big crowd gathered around some red posters so we went over to investigate.

"生命的路和墙"	The Road of Life and the Wall
世界上没有过这样的路	There is no such road in the world.
历史上也没有这样的墙	There is no such wall in history.
它是一条［？］救民主精英的路	It is a road to save the heroes of democracy.

它是一条繁民共铸钢铁的墙

It is a wall that is made of iron and steel and is built by all people.

这路上没有红灯[lü]灯

There are no traffic lights on this road.

走与[?]的信号是救护车的悲唱。

The signals are the wailing of ambulance sirens.

过去，

In the past,

因为它太坎坷，难走

because the road was rough and hard to walk on

我们只希望小平。

we only hoped for a bit of level ground[12].

现在我们觉醒了。

Now we are awake.

不要小平

We don't want "level ground"

而要康庄

We want the broad road.

[12] Xiaoping 小平 "a bit of level ground" is a play on the name [Deng] Xiaoping

这条墙是一条护路的墙	The wall is a wall that protects the road.
由畏惧	Because of fear
我们寄希望于幻想	we put our hope in fantasy.
现在我们勇敢了	Now we have become brave.
折离棚	Only by taking down the tent[13]
道路才更加宽广	can we widen the road.

岂有此李！？！	How could there be such nonsense!?! [In response to Li Peng on CCTV]

---

[13] Peng棚 (tent) is a play on the name [Li] Peng.

毛泽东部下 　敢打敢冲。	Mao's troops 　Dared to fight and charge
华国锋部下 　无影无踪。	Hua Guofeng's troops 　Disappeared without a trace.
邓小平部下 　百万富翁。	Deng Xiao Ping's troops 　Are a bunch of old millionaires.

毛泽东象太阳 照到哪里哪里亮 邓小平象月亮 初一十五不一样！	Mao Zedong was like the sun, Where he shone, there was light. Deng Xiaoping is like the moon, Not the same on the 1st and the 15th!

The Envelope for a Letter from Heaven

1003

寄北京中南海250 李鹏（儿）收 天堂政[?]真理路	To: Beijing Zhongnanhai 250[14] Recipient: Li Peng (son) Celestial Administration, Truth Road

天堂来信

啊鹏吾儿；
　见信如晤！

---

[14] 250 is slang for an idiot

天堂生活已十又三载，事务繁忙。近偶得闲暇又闻故土掀起狂澜，顿起下凡之心，于昨日魂归长安，察见数千学子绝食请愿，且闻广大市民怨声载道。甚感忧患，来克想我辈之大业竟衰汝等之手，将吾数十年之教诲付诸东流，痛哉！

以讲之才，本望汝作一普通公民，不指望汝当副处级以上干部，不想裙带之风竟将汝刮上总理之地位。而又与小平尚昆等人沆瀣一气黑暗神州！

法国留学之时，祝小平如兄弟，关心，教导于他，怎知他以八五寿居高位[?]忘民忧，未认其为人，保护，乃至，提[?]他一诚吾之失策，汝虽聪明有限，然仍居高级知识分子列，实不该为小平等人所利用，与人民为敌。铸成大错，鸣呼！

鹏儿，[？？？？] 犹未晚，金盆洗手还有时。辞去汝之所有官职，回到人民中去重新做人。否则，汝声明扫地。。。[？？？？？？？]

吾儿，回头是岸，不然百年之后，以汝之功德唯地狱之门向地敞开日。为父在天堂虽位居要职,[?]不能开此后门让汝升天！

朗朗晴空昭？吾之良苦？心？盼吾儿?会，吾儿自重。

此致。
父恩来字

五．二十

A Letter From Heaven

My dear son Peng,

May this letter be like a visit from me!

I have resided in heaven for thirteen years now, where I am busily engaged in numerous duties. Recently I chanced to find myself at leisure, and also to hear of great waves back in my home country, so I resolved to descend to the mortal realm. Yesterday my soul traveled back to the Old Capital, where I discovered that thousands of scholars were hunger striking and petitioning, and that cries of discontent were rising from the citizenry everywhere. I was deeply saddened, especially as my thoughts turned to how you and your associates, to whom I entrusted my generation's grand cause, have thrown my decades of instruction to the winds. Ah, woe is me!

With regard to talent, I always hoped that you would be a common citizen and did not anticipate that you would rise higher than a deputy bureau chief. I certainly did not expect the winds of nepotism to carry you all the way to the position of prime minister. Now you, along with Xiaoping and Shangkun, have brought darkness to the Divine Land!

When I studied abroad in France, I treated Xiaoping like a brother; I looked after him and guided him, never imagining that, at the ripe old age of 85, he would occupy such an exalted position and forget about the people's suffering. I did not know him for what he was! I protected him and even [promoted] him; verily, this was my mistake. Although you are of limited intelligence, you are nonetheless a member of the intelligentsia and should not have been manipulated by Xiaoping and his ilk into becoming an enemy of the people. Alas, I have committed a grave error!

Peng, my son, [?] it is not too late to stop; there is still time to wash your hands in the golden basin. Renounce all of your official titles, return to the people, and become a new person. If you do not, your reputation will drag in the dirt [transcription is unreadable here].

My son, come back to this side lest, one hundred years hence, on the basis of your merit, only the gates of hell will open for you. Even though your father is in a key position in the celestial realm, even I will not be able to open a back door to allow you to ascend to heaven.

As the bright sky illumines my vexed heart, I hope my son will understand, and will conduct himself with dignity!

Sincerely,
Your father Enlai. 5.20

Sally has stopped recording the contents of posters. She was previously asked to stop by a Waiban staffer and ignored it but today a guy in a sport coat with dark sunglasses, probably an undercover policeman, told her to stop.

∞∞∞∞∞∞∞∞∞

I asked a Chinese teacher I knew about one of the posters. He looked reluctant to talk, then said "Maybe Chinese aren't supposed to talk to foreigners." This was a polite way of saying that he wasn't going to talk to me since Chinese seen talking to foreigners could get into trouble.

As I walked back to the Foreigner's compound, I met a student I know well who is generally very talkative. He told me there was a fire in one of the dormitories but he didn't know any details. I asked him if people were really not supposed to talk to foreigners. He said "The situation is very serious in China. The situation is very serious in Beijing. Not so much here [Changchun], but it is still serious. If a policeman saw a person talking to a student, what would they think? You're a good person, but the policeman might not know that."

Now I'm worried that we will become isolated from the students. Will we stop hearing their news and their opinions about what's going on in China?

A few minutes later, two fire engines roared by on the street behind our building followed by dozens of running students. Sally and I ran out of our apartment building to see where they were going and Sally joined the group that was chasing the fire engines. Sally and the rest of the fire engine chasers came walking back a few minutes later, however, because the fire engines were actually driving off campus to their next fire.

When I met her outside the foreigner's compound fence, students who wanted to talk about the latest news quickly surrounded Sally and me. Apparently talking in a group to foreigners is okay since no student can be singled out.

One student told us that many of his friends couldn't sleep last night after hearing Li Peng's speech. The students are worried about the safety of the Beijing students and about China's future. They asked if I heard anything new today on VOA. I said I had nothing new to report.

Several students wondered how VOA or BBC will get news from China now that the international press can't send reports out of China using the satellite links and the international phone lines. They are worried that the foreign press will have to rely on official Chinese press reports that misrepresent the Democracy Movement.

All around us students were talking quietly in small groups. Sally heard someone say that six people died in Beijing yesterday. A teacher standing with us said that thirty-eight PLA commanders had resigned in Beijing rather than order their troops to attack the students.

∞∞∞∞∞∞∞∞∞

About 10 p.m., we started to hear chanting all around us. Students on the neighboring Northeast Teachers campus were yelling out their dorm windows, Jilin Tech students were chanting in the nearby Auto commons area, and large groups of students were singing and chanting as they crossed between the dorm areas.

I stood just outside our front door, listening to the students' voices echoing off the big library building a block behind our building and the Foreign Students Dorm in front of us. I was unable to distinguish one chant or song from another but I knew that sound contained all the students' anger, frustration, and fear.

The BBC evening shortwave broadcast reported that the Chinese government turned off the water in the Tiananmen area. I thought the government was concerned about the student's welfare!

The CCTV news in English announced that foreigners are not allowed to engage in activities against martial law, including spreading rumors.

At around 10:30 p.m., the noise coming from the Northeast Teachers campus grew to an angry roar. Sally decided to see what was going on and slipped into the pitch black darkness outside our compound while I stood in our doorway, worrying that something bad would happen out there. Sally returned after what seemed like a long time (it was probably just a few minutes) and told me that the noise was the Northeast Teachers students in the dorm next to our campus venting their anger at the government and their school's administration.

5/21 Sunday

Last night, Jilin Tech student representatives went to Xinfa Circle to help plan a city-wide student march for today.

This morning VOA reported that students and Beijing residents stopped troops from advancing toward Tiananmen yesterday. I guess the army is still not ready to roll over people to reach the Square.

About 10 a.m., a large group of Jilin Tech students marched down the street behind our apartment building. They were carrying handmade banners, some with just the school's name and some with demands like "Li Peng Out." The fancy department banners they used in the first demonstrations were nowhere in sight, probably back in the closet now since these demonstrations cannot be officially sponsored.

It was my turn to go with the student march, so I climbed over the compound fence (to avoid going by the guard at the compound gate who records our comings and goings), hopped on the bike we left outside the fence, and followed the marching students. I assumed that martial law or at least much greater police scrutiny was in effect in Changchun so I rode on the sidewalk near the back of the march, far enough from the students to not be part of the march but close enough to see what was going on.

Stalin Boulevard was packed with the usual Sunday crowd of shoppers and families going to the parks. Sunday is the only day off work in China and people seemed to be doing the normal Sunday activities regardless of the turmoil in Beijing.

I decided to ride past the Jilin Tech march so I could see what was going on further up Stalin. When I reached Peoples Circle, I saw a crowd gathered around a large stage on the north side of the park inside the circle. I rode toward the stage thinking there was a student rally going on there but when I got there I was shocked to find myself at the Changchun city workers aerobic dance contest, where a performance by twenty or thirty street sweepers was in progress.[15] It was unbelievable that city officials would be spending time today judging the aerobic dance styles of the city workers while a huge struggle for democracy was going on in China! The dancing was kind of mesmerizing, however, and I stayed and watched until the street sweepers finished their routine.

When the Jilin Tech student march reached People's Circle, I saw that it was smaller than I expected, maybe 3,000 to 4,000 people and quieter than the previous marches.

The marchers were organized into short, straight rows, everyone in a row holding hands with the person beside them. The march was preceded by several rows of students walking bikes that could be dropped to the ground to prevent a police attack from the front. There were, however, only a few police in

---

[15] The street sweepers were women that swept the streets with brooms.

the area, most of them directing traffic.

I followed the marchers as they continued up Stalin past the aerobics competition and onto the busy stretch near Department Store #5. Young people and students on the sidewalks joined the march until it filled the street. I could feel the anger and excitement of the marchers rising as they approached the provincial government building at Xinfa Circle. When I looked behind me, I saw a number of people reading the leaflets the students handed out.

The marchers continued past the provincial government building and turned west onto a street that led away from the circle. I decided not to follow them so I headed back down Stalin toward home. About halfway home, I heard cheering and shouting to the west so I turned and headed toward the Jilin University campus. When I got to the Jilin University main gate, I saw a few dozen students cheering as other students put up posters that I think contained news updates and photos from Changchun demonstrations. The crowd grew steadily in the next few minutes and began to spill into the street but the police made no attempt to move them. I decided to head home.

When I got to the apartment, I listened to the BBC afternoon news. PLA troops were still on the outskirts of Beijing, waiting for orders to advance to Tiananmen. It was clear the military had not yet decided to overrun the barricades and attack the students.

Some students think the PLA troops might be advancing on Tiananmen through the subway tunnels that ring central Beijing. Troops moving through these tunnels could avoid the roadblocks and student squads and attack the square without warning.

∞∞∞∞∞∞∞∞∞

Around dinnertime some students told us that the army had captured Tiananmen, injuring many people in the process. Could that be true? It was depressing to think the army would break through the people's blockade and attack the students!

I talked with some friends who grew up during the Cultural Revolution. They think the troops will clear the square and disperse the students but the students will be back again in the future. I think they're right.

The CCTV news at 7 p.m. brought good and bad news. The army did not advance to Tiananmen today but the army headquarters announced that they will clear Tiananmen without delay.

The most incredible thing about the CCTV news broadcast was the attitude of the announcers--a young man and woman. The other day these same announcers calmly read the martial law decree but tonight they were clearly very upset. They both spoke more slowly than usual and the male announcer read the military command's statement about Tiananmen with obvious distaste, pausing sometimes as if he could not go on, and once even flicking away one of his sheets of paper when he finished reading it. The female announcer's voice was barely audible as she read her part of the report. I think this was an act of civil disobedience. I bet the police are questioning those announcers right now.

About ten we heard chanting, clapping, and yelling from the Northeast Teachers campus, but I don't know why they were making all that noise.

I think the Democracy Movement is almost over because it sounds like the army will do whatever they have to in order to clear the square. We prepared lesson plans for the next morning's classes because we thought the strike might be over.

5/22 Monday

When I woke up I hurried downstairs so I would be sure to hear the VOA morning broadcast. VOA says the students are still on Tiananmen!!

I walked to Classroom Building #1 to teach my first class. When I stopped by the teacher's lounge on my way to the classroom, the teachers told me that the strike is still on and they would not teach if there were only a few students present.

There were two girls sitting in my classroom when I got there, good students who probably came to get some extra English practice. I sat down with them and we talked in English about my kids and about how hard it was for me to learn Chinese. Three boy students came to the door, looked around the room, and then came in and sat down next to the girls. The boys wouldn't talk and looked especially nervous when the girls started telling me about the latest news from Beijing. I looked outside and said the weather was nice so we ought to go enjoy the day. Everyone agreed and we left.

I left Classroom Building #1 and wandered over to "Democracy Wall," a wall of one of the Automobile Department dorms that was now covered with handmade posters containing news and opinions.[16] I

---

[16] This wall was named after the original Democracy Wall on Xidan Street in Beijing where people posted messages of democratic

chatted with some students about the latest news and then went home.

Democracy Wall on an Auto Dorm

At noon, CCTV news reported that the situation in Beijing is chaotic and again warned citizens not to participate in anti-government activities. The announcers read a statement from the army that said that their mission is to look for a few bad people who are behind the chaos and that no innocent people will be harmed.

During that news broadcast there was an interview with an army officer who said the students had stopped his soldiers' progress into the city. He said he's been told that the situation in Beijing is extremely bad and his troops will have to fight anyone who blocks them if he is ordered to get his troops into the city to quell the disorder.

---

dissent in December 1978 during the period known as the Beijing Spring. That Democracy Wall was shut down in 1979 when the postings on the wall began to openly criticize the Communist Party and the government.

What was really striking was the video for the story. If you looked behind the officer as he was being interviewed, you could see several army trucks surrounded by people. You could also see students sitting on the trucks, peacefully talking and eating with the soldiers.

Who let this video be shown on the carefully controlled national TV news? Are there people running the media who secretly support the students' demands? I'm following the lead of my students who say that they always read between the lines of the government broadcasts to try to figure out the truth.

∞∞∞∞∞∞∞∞∞∞

This afternoon, I spoke with some students who had just returned from Beijing. They told me that the student movement on Tiananmen is very organized and the movement leaders are in control of the nationwide movement. They say the CCTV news' claims of serious disruption and looting in the city are untrue.

One returned student told me about a conversation with a farmer during one of the marches. The farmer asked him, "What is this democracy you're talking about?" The student told the farmer that in a democracy the government does what the people want, not what the leaders want. I didn't hear whether the farmer liked that definition.

Another student told a story about a confrontation with soldiers that was witnessed by his friend. In the story, a group of students stopped an army convoy by lying down in front of the trucks and then letting the air out of the truck tires. While the students were explaining their demands to the stranded soldiers, they saw tear gas canisters in the back of the truck. The students asked the soldiers if they knew what the canisters were for and the soldiers said no. The students explained that they were tear gas for attacking crowds like the students on Tiananmen. The students said the soldiers cried when they heard what they were going to be ordered to do.

∞∞∞∞∞∞∞∞

A very enthusiastic young male newsreader was the cohost of the CCTV news tonight in place of the guy that was mad/depressed last night. The female newsreader from last night was there but she didn't look as depressed.

Sally went to a late-night student meeting in front of the big Jilin Tech auditorium where it was announced that the student strike will continue. Tomorrow at 9 a.m. the students will march to a citywide coalition meeting.

∞∞∞∞∞∞∞∞

Letter Home Excerpt (Sent 5/22/89)

Dear Mom,

...As far as what's going on here, we're all basically waiting for something to happen in Beijing. I'm sure by now (the time you read this letter) the confrontation will be resolved but for now we have no idea what will happen.

Changchun is very quiet except for the campuses. All the schools, including ours, are on strike and marches are held up Stalin Boulevard every day or two. The people in the city are very responsive to the protesters' demands about corruption, freedom of the press, etc. There are no full-scale strikes or riots like Beijing, however, and the police allow all the demonstrations to continue without interruption. Our news all comes from Voice of America and the BBC or from some word of mouth. Most students avoid us now since in Beijing the Chinese are not allowed to speak to foreigners if they are "spreading rumors." Not fun.

So we are somewhat isolated and not teaching. We have to start preparing to leave but the feeling here is that everything is on hold. We're certainly hoping for a quick resolution—a favorable resolution—so we can finish teaching and go…

I'd write more on the situation but I don't know if it's advisable. You'll hear about it soon enough.

Jay

5/23 Tuesday

VOA reported that troops broke through some of the people's barricades last night but they did not advance all the way to Tiananmen. So the PLA did attack the people! The students are still on Tiananmen but this advance by the army shows that they may not be safe there for long.

I heard that students who are Party members were told to start attending classes today. I'm only teaching undergrads this semester and I don't think many undergrads are Party members so that won't affect the attendance in my classes but attendance may go up in graduate student classes.

∞∞∞∞∞∞∞∞

When I reported to my undergraduate conversation class at 8 a.m. the classroom was empty. In fact, all the rooms in Classroom Building #1 were empty.

I talked to someone from the Foreign Languages department while I was leaving the classroom building. That person told me my family should be careful because things could get dangerous in Changchun. I said we would.

∞∞∞∞∞∞∞∞

About two to three thousand Jilin Tech students

gathered a little later than planned for today's march. The group carried banners and signs with student demands, including the demand that Li Peng resign from his posts. I had seen a larger Northeast Teachers march leave their campus earlier in the day.

As we watched the march form up, a graduate student I know came up to say hello. He said he had supported the movement until two days ago, but he would not march today because the students were going too far when they called for the overthrow of the government. I think he's a Communist Party member since his statements sounded like the official Party line.

The student coalition decided to make today "Win Public Support Day." Students from many schools mobbed the busy area from People's Circle to Xinfa Circle to spread the news about what's really going on in Beijing and to ask people to support the student movement. They talked one-on-one with people on the street, made speeches to larger groups of people on the Circle, and plastered the downtown area with posters containing news from Beijing. I saw two Jilin Tech students give a tearful plea at Xinfa Circle that visibly moved the crowd.

∞∞∞∞∞∞∞∞∞

I heard today that the Democracy Movement coalition of schools in Changchun—16 universities and institutes that have over 20,000 students—is now part of a nationwide network of students led by the Beijing student leaders. Every day the student leaders in Beijing will call city coalition leaders and tell them what kind of activities to plan for the next day. Every night at 8:30 p.m., each school will hold a meeting on their campus to announce the next day's activities.

I also heard today that more Changchun students are leaving for Beijing. All the students who went to Beijing last Thursday and Friday are back, but the Beijing students put out a call for more supporters to come to Tiananmen. This is in direct opposition to the government's call for students to return to their campuses.

The nightly CCTV news showed pictures of huge rallies on Tiananmen supporting the students' demands. This is the first time I've seen video of a Beijing student demonstration on CCTV--has the media loosened up because of outrage over the obvious censorship of Democracy Movement news?

I heard a rumor that CCTV reporters are protesting the occupation of the CCTV studios by PLA troops. I bet the newsreader who looked so disgusted the other day is protesting!

5/24 Wednesday

The VOA morning broadcast says the students are still camped out on Tiananmen and the PLA troops are still mainly on the outskirts of the city. I think a furious power struggle is raging within the government and army about how to proceed.

I went to my 8:00 a.m. class expecting to find an empty classroom. There were five students, however, and they wanted to stay. I didn't have a lesson prepared so I decided just to sit and talk with them.

I started the discussion by asking them what they would do this summer, but we wound up discussing democracy in the US. One student asked: "If students have a march on campus and raise some demands, does the university respond to the students' demands right away? Does the university president meet with the protesting students?" I gave a long answer that mainly boiled down to "No, not really." They responded by saying that in the democracy they would like to have in China, the school would have to respond right away to student demands.

The discussion moved to free speech and I explained how in the US you usually could say whatever you wanted about a university or the government, but it didn't get published in the newspaper unless the newspaper's editors and owners chose to print it.

One student asked me what Americans think about

U.S. college students. I answered that there are many different attitudes among Americans toward college students and the attitudes have changed over time. That's in stark contrast to the uniformly positive attitude toward university students in China. In fact, most people refer to the university students as "our students."

The students then told me about life in the Chinese countryside. I know unemployment is very high there and public education is crumbling but they told me about serious problems with crime and violence. One student told me about a 2000-member robber band that terrorized the area he grew up in until the police caught the leader. Another student told me about a fight between gangs of school children where one was killed and several seriously injured. He said these young people were frustrated and angry because they were not doing well in school and knew their futures were going to be difficult.

∞∞∞∞∞∞∞∞

This afternoon, some of Sally's students who had just returned from Beijing came to tell us about their experiences and to show us some Beijing newspaper clippings.

They told us that the people of Beijing are giving the students amazing support. People offered these students rides to wherever they were going and the bus conductors let them ride for free. They said restaurants are giving food to students for free or at reduced prices.

They told us that the residents of Beijing have donated an average of 80 yuan a family to the Beijing

73

students and some families gave up to 1000 yuan. [17] That's very generous since the average monthly salary in China is around 120 yuan. The motto of the students for Beijingers was "If you have money, give us money. If you have no money, give us your strength. If you have no strength, make us some porridge." The students said there was a constant stream of people bringing food to Tiananmen.

The students told us a story about a confrontation between Beijingers and soldiers advancing on Beijing. One day some of the male Jilin Tech students were part of a group of students sent to stop advancing soldiers. When the students reached the troops they saw that an old man and woman had already stopped the column by lying down in the street in front of the lead truck. The old couple told the soldiers that they would have to drive over them if they wanted to attack the students.

The students found out that some soldiers were told they were going to Beijing for maneuvers while others were told they were going there to make a movie. The student said the soldiers cried when they read Beijing newspapers the students gave them and saw that the army was brought to Beijing to attack the students.

The students we were talking with said that the health of the hunger strikers, some of the best and brightest students in China, is permanently damaged and they probably won't continue their studies. The least affected hunger strikers are still on Tiananmen Square but the weakest are in the hospital.

They told the story of one hunger striker that refused

[17] In 1989 one yuan was worth about 12 US cents.

to drink water. His mother and brother came to Tiananmen to plead with him to drink, saying that he must live to see their victory and democracy in China but he still refused. Our students don't know what happened to him.

The students were on Tiananmen on May 20th when martial law was declared. They said they stayed awake all night waiting for an attack by troops or police but nothing happened.

They said that everyone in Beijing is calling Deng Xiaoping the new Emperor and they are wondering why Chinese leaders all end up acting like emperors. The Beijing students have come up with ideas to stop one person or a small group of people from controlling the country, ideas that include creating new government oversight bodies and strengthening the rubber-stamp New People's Congress so its members could control or veto the decisions of the leaders.

The students told us that people are saying "If Mao was the sun, then Deng is the moon because he's never the same on the 1st and the 15th."[18]

They also said people are contrasting the current Democracy Movement with the May 4th Movement, an anti-imperialist movement sparked by student demonstrations in Beijing on May 4, 1919. People are saying that the May 4th Movement was aimed at saving China from foreign control but the current Democracy Movement is centered on establishing democracy in China.

---

[18] A popular propaganda slogan said that Mao was the red sun in the people's hearts

The students said that 600 Jilin Tech students went to Beijing over three days last week but most of them returned over the following three days when the Communist Party ordered their student members to return to their schools.

Students are still going to Beijing, though. I heard that last night's train to Beijing was full (which means absolutely crammed full) so some people had to wait for the morning train.

As I'm writing this I can hear the shouts and cheers from the nightly student meeting.

5/25 Thursday

This morning VOA reported that the army did not push through the city to Tiananmen last night. VOA speculates that there's a struggle going on between the people favoring repression (championed by Li Peng but with Deng Xiaoping in charge) and those favoring political reform (led by Zhao Ziyang). I think the students are fighting for political reforms—a more democratic country—but not for the economic reforms that Zhao has championed because those reforms are leading to the widespread inequality that the students hate.

VOA also said that the Chinese government cut the satellite links out of China. We've heard that before, but maybe the earlier announcements were just threats.

I went to Classroom Building #1 for my first scheduled class but the classrooms were all empty. I stopped by the teacher's lounge and listened for a while as the teachers talked openly about strengthening the strike.

Even though everyone's spirits are high right now, I'm not sure how long our students can maintain the strike. Is this level of enthusiasm enough to keep students involved when the government is taking such a hard line against the movement? Will the Jilin Tech administration start threatening the striking students with expulsion?

Since I didn't have to teach a class today, I rode my bike downtown to see what was going on. Everything looked fairly normal with two exceptions.

First, I saw large handmade posters placed at strategic spots along Stalin Boulevard all the way to downtown. Wherever there were posters, there were people reading them, some of them standing, some sitting on their bikes, and some trying to read the posters as they drove by them. I could also see places where posters were recently torn down.

Second, the police were present in small numbers at all the major intersections, watching the people moving by them and talking quietly on their radios. The only time I saw them move from their posts was to arrest a derelict that had broken all the glass in a building door with a metal rod.

When I got back to Jilin Tech, the campus was quiet. Someone told me that a lot of students had gone to the Changchun #1 Auto Plant to try and convince the 100,000 autoworkers to support the Democracy Movement.

I think the auto factory is fertile ground for organizing by the students. A Changchun autoworker I met recently told me that, except for a few official union leaders, the workers support the student demands. Reaching out to workers for support is a nationwide policy of the student movement, a policy meant to broaden the movement and give it more power.

∞∞∞∞∞∞∞∞

Apparently some Communist Party members at Jilin Tech put up posters that criticized the Party leaders' attacks on the student movement. That's a violation of Communist Party rules—rank and file Party members are not allowed to publicly disagree with the decisions of the Party Central Committee. We heard that other Party members are tearing down those posters.

∞∞∞∞∞∞∞∞

The CCTV nightly news featured Li Peng giving a speech to some assembled cadre. He must still be in control of the government.

The students' nightly meeting is spirited again. We can hear a lot of cheering and shouting.

5/26 Friday

The VOA morning broadcast gave a complete report on Li Peng's speech. Li said that the demonstrators may be honest but they don't understand the situation in China. He said the government never wanted to bring troops to Beijing but they were forced to do it. Now, Li said, China is being criticized by foreigners who don't understand that martial law means something different in China than it does in other countries. Li stated that Deng Xiaoping is the real reformer in China.

In the late morning a student who has just returned from Beijing told me that five hunger strikers have died and more are comatose. Apparently many of the hunger strikers prepared for death by making wills and sending last letters to their family and friends. One Jilin Tech hunger striker called a fellow teacher and told her that if he died, his roommate would bring over some pictures that he wanted her to have. He told her that he loved her, and said goodbye.

∞∞∞∞∞∞∞∞∞

There's terrible news on the BBC afternoon broadcast—Zhao Ziyang and Wan Li have been denounced as plotters against the government! [19]

---

[19] In 1989, Wan Li was Chairman of the National People's Congress, the only legislative body in China. A supporter of Hu Yaobang and Zhao Ziyang's economic and political policies, Wan was in Canada

80

Other Party leaders who have sided with Zhao are under house arrest and more troops are being moved to Beijing to stamp out what is now being called "the plot."

Deng Xiaoping, once denounced as a counterrevolutionary by Mao Zedong, is applying the same label to the leaders who have shown some sympathy for the student movement. Is there anything the Chinese people can do about this? Will the troops attack the students now that the Party leaders who tolerated the Democracy Movement are denounced as counter-revolutionaries?

The BBC reports that the students camped on Tiananmen Square have decided to stay there which means they'll almost certainly come face to face with PLA troops in the near future.

I went over to the Jilin Tech Democracy Wall to get the latest news from the students. A student there told me that two hundred Jilin Tech students are on Tiananmen Square and the school was specifically named on VOA as strongly supporting the Beijing students. What a change from a few weeks ago when our students were uninvolved!

I heard that since the strike started many Jilin Tech students were ordered to come home by their worried parents. A student told me that many dorms are almost empty—that's why the campus is so quiet.

---

in May 1989, where he made some speeches sympathetic to the Beijing students. He was expected to return to Beijing in late May but instead he flew to Shanghai where he may have been under house arrest.

5/27 Saturday

The VOA morning news broadcast reported that the conservative bloc of Party leaders have ordered the arrest of the Party leaders sympathetic to the student movement and have taken control of the government. They announced that the entire Party leadership would meet soon to ratify these emergency decisions.

My first class today was half full but the students didn't bring their books. Before I started teaching the lesson I said they could leave if they wanted. Everyone stayed.

First, we played a conversation game that I thought they would like and then I talked about democracy in the US. They were very interested in my description of American democracy but they listened critically and had questions that indicated that the US government wasn't as responsive to people's concerns as they thought a democratic government should be.

After class I talked to friends outside the building who said they expected the conservative leaders to start punishing anyone who has participated in the student movement. Will any of our students be expelled because of their participation? Will they be thrown into jail?

Today the Jilin Tech administration announced that

they will expel students who aren't back in class in three days. Will they follow through on that threat?

They also announced that Jilin Tech seniors and graduate students will be allowed to graduate even though the spring semester probably won't be completed. That's great news for students that are supposed to finish this year but there could be problems ahead for graduating students that were involved in the student movement. The university and the associated government ministry give each graduate a mandatory job assignment and those administrators could assign activist students to undesirable jobs or to jobs in an undesirable location in China.

Students who don't accept their job assignment and go to work somewhere else won't have an official residence registration. The residence registration qualifies people for free housing and medical care in their registered location, close to their workplace. You don't need a residence registration in the new free enterprise zones like Shenzhen in southern China but that path is probably only for students who think they would prosper in the new free market economy.

The Jilin University students declared yesterday to be Truth Day and marched up to People's Circle to spread the news about what is really happening in Beijing. Sally reported that a large crowd gathered on the circle applauded a student's speech decrying the victory of the conservatives. Several hundred police positioned around the circle watched all the activity.

∞∞∞∞∞∞∞∞

The CCTV nightly news repeated the new Party line on the democracy movement. They said the movement is a plot against the Chinese Party and government led by "very, very few" people who are all now in custody.

5/28 Sunday

This morning, VOA reported that the students will leave Tiananmen after holding mass marches there today and Tuesday.

I agree with the student decision to leave Tiananmen. The government is not going to negotiate with the students about reform now that those demands are associated with the so-called counter-revolutionary plot. We will get some eyewitness reports about the final days on Tiananmen from Jilin Tech students who are there now.

After lunch I saw a small group of students marching around campus, chanting and waving at the other students. I learned later this march was in response to a call by the Beijing students for Chinese all over the world to march today for democracy.

When I went out to watch the marchers pass by our compound, I met a student who I was pretty sure was a Party member. He was watching the marchers and grinning but he sounded cynical as he said "Oh, so you're here to experience the student feeling." On the topic of the Beijing students, he said that the government was handling them gently, letting other forces push them back to classes. He called the government's handling of the students "very skillful."

∞∞∞∞∞∞∞∞∞∞

About 10 p.m. the chanting all around us got much louder. When I went outside to see what was going on, I heard students in the Auto Dorms commons chanting "Yi, Er, Bake!" (One, Two, Strike). I think the loud strike chants were in response to signs posted today by the Jilin Tech administration stating that they HOPED students would return to class the next morning. The character for Hope was written larger than the other characters on the sign.

I went outside again a half hour later when I heard the sounds of a large crowd moving across campus. Students marching shoulder-to-shoulder were surging out of the Auto dorm commons onto the street that ran behind our compound. I hopped over the compound fence and joined the march just as the students broke into a spirited singing of the Internationale. I was moved by their spirit and determination in the face of a certain government crackdown.

After a few blocks I stepped out of the march onto the sidewalk and watched them continue on toward the Great Hall for their nightly meeting. A student stepped out of the march and told me that they were going to be told tonight whether Changchun students are supposed to stay on strike until the Beijing students return to their classes. The student said that after the meeting on our campus they will probably go to the Northeast Teachers campus and maybe to a bigger meeting at Xinfa Circle.

The Jilin Tech students marched off campus at some point but student voices echoed around us for a long time. Sometime around midnight I heard the students, chanting loudly, march back onto campus.

5/29 Monday

I saw a lot of students going into Classroom Building #1 as I rode my bike up to the building. As I walked down the hall to my classroom I saw that all the classes had at least five or six students and some had as many as twelve or thirteen—less than the twenty to thirty of a full class but definitely the most students in class since the strike began. When I entered my classroom the six or seven students waiting for me seemed attentive and ready for class. When I asked if they would rather be in class or on strike, one or two students said they wanted to strike and most of them nodded their heads in agreement but no one left the room.

Since I hadn't prepared a lesson, I suggested that we have a discussion in English. The students started the discussion by asking me what I thought about the current situation in China. I turned it around and asked how they felt and they said they supported the strike but their spirits were low. They said they were puzzled why a government that says it has the same goals as the Beijing students refuses to talk with the students. We discussed reports they had heard about cases of paralysis and mental illness among the hunger strikers, but we all agreed that those reports might just be rumors.

Someone said the Jilin Tech administration announced there will be no reprisals against student strikers. Another student said the school made the same announcement during student demonstrations in 1979 but they expelled the student leaders six months after the demonstrations ended.

The students said they had also heard that Zhao Ziyang was under house arrest in his hometown of Chengdu. They said that many other Party leaders have been arrested.

Students brought up the subject of guandao, the practice of high officials or their relatives getting rich by abusing their privileges and connections. They said this is a serious problem in China and that Deng Xiaoping's son was the biggest guandao around. They agreed that he had a hard time during the Cultural Revolution when he lost his legs, but they say he's rich now and involved in all kinds of shady businesses.

Another student told a story about army troops advancing on Tiananmen. The troops, stopped nonviolently by students, were ordered not to talk to the students or read the newspapers the students were handing out. The soldiers got the newspapers on the sly, read the news, and were won over to the students' point of view. Later, when police attacked students in front of those soldiers, the soldiers pointed their guns at the police and ordered them to leave the students alone.

A student felt it was important for me to understand the differences between the Cultural Revolution and this student movement. The student said the Cultural Revolution was a top-down movement directed by Mao Zedong and the Gang of Four but the Democracy Movement is a real bottom-up people's movement.

The students told me that some Beijing students want to stay on Tiananmen Square until June 20, the opening of the New People's Congress. The NPC is the only legislative body in the People's Republic of China and it could, theoretically, reverse or at least openly question the actions of the government against the students and the arrested Party leaders.

The 8 a.m. class ended and I waited in the classroom for the students in my 10 a.m. class but no one showed up. Later in the day I found out why so many students came to the 8 a.m. classes. Last night, Jilin Tech department heads and professors went to the dormitories and told the students that the demonstrations are over so they better go back to class. Faculty members went to the dorms again this morning, woke the students up, and made sure they left for their 8 a.m. classes on time.

One student told me that four teachers came to his room to make sure that he and his roommates were getting ready for class. The teachers told them they would call roll in class--if the students weren't there it would be a black mark against them. No one was threatened with expulsion so it sounded like a mild threat.

I heard later that many students rebelled against this faculty pressure to attend class by going to the wrong classroom building or going to the right building but the wrong room. Also, students who went to the 8 a.m. class made themselves scarce after class so the university authorities couldn't force them to go to their next class.

5/30 Tuesday

We didn't teach today but I checked inside Classroom Building #1 and saw a few students in every classroom.

The VOA morning news reported that the student leaders on Tiananmen disagree on when to leave the square. Some say they are going to stay there until June 20 and some say they will leave Tiananmen soon and use different tactics to reach their goals.

VOA also reported that a group of students is erecting a large replica of the Statue of Liberty on Tiananmen. I think that's probably a mistake since it will leave them open to charges of foreign influence on the movement.

∞∞∞∞∞∞∞∞∞∞

We talked with a student who just returned from Beijing. The student said the people of Beijing are still providing amazing support for the students. He also said that the leadership of the students was changing every two or three days as a result of disagreements about what to do next but the movement remains well organized. He said many students in Beijing are talking about going back to their campuses.

The student said that photographers and reporters from Western news outlets are visiting Tiananmen regularly but reporters from Chinese news organizations are not allowed to go to the square. As one teacher said a few days ago, people living outside

China are seeing a lot more of what's going on in Beijing than we are and we're only 750 miles away from there.

∞∞∞∞∞∞∞∞

There is a rumor that the Jilin Tech class monitors told the school's administrators which students are in Beijing.[20] The rumor started because the Jilin Tech administration recently sent telegrams to inform parents that their children are participating in the student movement and are on Tiananmen Square.

Today we also heard the shocking news that three to five thousand of China's leading intellectuals have pledged to go on a hunger strike to force the government to address the students' demands.

∞∞∞∞∞∞∞∞

The nightly CCTV news was full of criticisms of the Statue of Liberty that the students built on Tiananmen. The CCTV news emphasized how strange this statue is and showed interviews with people who said things like "This is China, not America." "What is some kind of goddess doing on Tiananmen?"

This was the first CCTV mention in a week of the students on Tiananmen.

∞∞∞∞∞∞∞∞

---

[20] Students have all their classes for all four years of school with the same group of 30-40 students. A monitor, appointed by the school, is that group's spokesperson but also the schools source of information on what the students are doing.

It's late now and our students should be at the nightly meeting but I don't hear any cheers or chants coming from the direction of the Great Hall.

I found out that they meet at night to better mask the identity of the students who lead the meeting. The meeting leaders also wear disguises and speak from the middle of the crowd.

5/31 Wednesday

This morning VOA reported that Chinese trade union leaders that have vocally supported the Democracy Movement are being arrested. The government didn't confirm or deny the arrests.

Last night Jilin Tech officials prevented the nightly student meeting from happening. They stood in front of the auditorium and told gathering students that the meeting was cancelled because the student leader was busy. Someone also tore down all the posters on campus again.

Preventing the meeting seems to have had an effect on the student's morale. My 8 a.m. class was the largest since the strike started and the 10 a.m. class was almost full attendance.

∞∞∞∞∞∞∞∞∞

We had a humorous experience with some Chinese workers on campus. I was walking with a few other teachers down a street next to our compound when we saw a group of men digging a trench (someone is always digging a trench somewhere on campus to fix the water pipes or the district heat pipes). When one teacher's wife asked a workman what the trench was for he replied that "it's a tunnel to America, we don't like it here anymore."

∞∞∞∞∞∞∞∞∞

The CCTV nightly news featured interviews with people who support the government's policy toward Zhao and the students. The broadcast also included video of pro-government demonstrations by farmers, demonstrations that I'm sure were staged by the government. The announcers also read letters of support for the government and letters of condemnation of the goddess on Tiananmen.

6/1 Thursday

There was full attendance in my class today and there were no Jilin Tech student meetings or rallies. Is the strike over?

6/2 Friday

The VOA morning report had bad news and good news. The bad news is that troops are slowly but surely moving through Beijing toward Tiananmen. Also, farmers burned an effigy of Fang Lizhi, a leading Chinese dissident, at a government sponsored rally against counterrevolutionaries.

The good news is that trade union leaders arrested earlier this week were released yesterday, following several days of large rallies demanding their freedom.

VOA says the US government has threatened reprisals against China if force is used against the students. What kind of action would the US take? Jilin Tech students who want to go to graduate school in the US are worried that diplomatic problems between the US and China will make it hard to get a student visa next year.

Last night CCTV news reported that students across the country do not support the Beijing students and to prove the point they stated that 90% of Jilin Tech students have returned to class. Some Jilin Tech students were really embarrassed by that, so they called a spot strike at noon and started harassing students who were heading to afternoon classes. The strike was effective—I heard that no students showed up for the afternoon or night classes.

I think Jilin Tech was mentioned on the news because they wanted to show that students at a school that was one of the most radical campuses during the Cultural Revolution were now supporting the government. During the wild years of the Cultural

Revolution, two revolutionary student factions emerged and turned the campus into an ideological and physical battleground. The army had to be called in to restore order and stop a running gun battle between students in Classroom Building #2 and their rivals in the library building.

6/3 Saturday

This morning, VOA reported that the army tried to move troops all the way to Tiananmen Square but they were stopped! A number of the fasting intellectuals are on the Square now and a workers organization has put up a big tent. In spite of all their threats of repression, the government has failed to stamp out the movement!

Some classrooms are full today and some are empty. Apparently, some of the class groups voted to strike while some groups voted to attend class.

Our foreign affairs people met with us today to discuss the current situation in China. They repeated the Party line about the movement being inspired by counterrevolutionaries and urged us to stay out of harm's way.

I heard from friends that in some Chinese cities people are being asked to sign loyalty oaths.

In their afternoon broadcast, the BBC reported that riot police fought with students who are occupying an area outside the Communist Party headquarters at Zhongnanhai, a heavily guarded compound a quarter mile west of Tiananmen Square. The government claims that the students attacked the troops guarding the compound, but I don't believe that's true.

I heard a rumor that Jilin Tech students were talking about leaving en masse before final exams, but I talked with another student who said the remaining students on campus really don't know what they should do.

We decided to go out for a family dinner at a Hui[21] restaurant next to nearby Nanhu Park. When we walked to the restaurant the streets were crowded with shoppers and people heading to the park for a walk--just a normal Saturday.

When we got home we turned on the TV and saw a special announcement scrolling across the bottom of the screen that said that two serious incidents had happened that day in Beijing. First, a gang of punks and hooligans had blocked troops from doing their jobs. The second incident was said to be at Zhongnanhai, probably the fighting the BBC described in their earlier broadcast. The announcement warned all Beijing residents that in order to protect themselves they should stay in their homes, not go to Tiananmen, or go out at all. Could this be the big push to get the students off Tiananmen? It must be.

A few minutes later, an American teacher called with an update. A nightly VOA broadcast reported that PLA troops are moving toward central Beijing again and are using force against anyone that gets in their way. We'll have to wait for tomorrow's news to find out more since that was the last VOA broadcast to China today.

The CCTV English news said that small groups were putting up posters on campuses calling on people to overthrow the government. They did not report on the troop movements.

---

[21] A Muslim ethnic group

6/4 Sunday

They did it. The Chinese army attacked Beijing with a vicious, full-scale assault. I am stunned, shocked, upset, and worried. Somehow I thought there would be a compromise.

VOA reports that last night troops shot their way through the citizen and student roadblocks and cleared Tiananmen Square, but there are no reports on what happened to the students that were on the Square. VOA reports that troops are driving through the city this morning, shooting people on the street and firing into apartment buildings. They say the Beijing hospitals are full of dead and wounded people and casualties are still streaming in.

Also this morning, the BBC reported that the army is shooting unarmed people on the streets of Beijing.

∞∞∞∞∞∞∞∞∞

We went out to Democracy Wall to get the latest news and to be with the students. They were milling around, listening to portable radios, and reading the latest posters on the wall. They are angry, sad, and shocked—they really didn't think that the PLA would attack Chinese. They are very worried about family and classmates in Beijing.

One teacher said "If they had just talked to the students two weeks ago, this would have been avoided. It doesn't make sense."

Some students are trying to organize a march through the city but a lot of students are afraid the police will attack the march.

Some students think that the Chinese people, except for the people in Beijing, will not outwardly oppose this brutal repression. As one teacher said "The people of Beijing are heroic but the people in the rest of China will watch and wait."

Most Chinese get all their news from the government-run radio and TV stations so they will only see and hear the government's version of what's happening in Beijing. Our students, however, listen to foreign shortwave broadcasts and get eyewitness reports from Beijing so they have access to a very different point of view. Only people in Beijing know the whole truth since they have watched the movement unfold and are now the victims of the violence.

This is another tremendous blow to the Chinese people's pride. One teacher said to me that "The eyes of the world are on China and this happens."

I was asked again about democracy in America and I pointed out its strengths and weaknesses. When they asked if the American government ever shot demonstrators, I told them that it had happened (for example, May 4th at Kent State) but it was rare. I said that police do use tear gas and clubs against demonstrators if the demonstration is considered to be illegal.

Students say that this is one of the few universities where students have not all gone home or to Beijing. The students I've talked with want to go home and end the year with an empty school strike, but they seem worried about leaving. I have a feeling most of the people that are still here will stay until the university officially postpones or cancels final exams.

Someone told me that the 27th PLA army group is responsible for most of the brutality in Beijing. When I repeated that to a friend, she said "Of course, it's the Yang Jia Jun" (Yang Family Army)—an PLA group with all Yang Shangkun's relatives in command.[22] Yang, one of the old guard of the Party, has thrown his support behind Deng and the crackdown.

The CCTV midday news presented the government version of the PLA's attack on Beijing. CCTV reported that soldiers were sent into Beijing to put down the counterrevolution led by Zhao Ziyang. They said that many of those soldiers were injured battling the counterrevolutionaries and many citizens were hurt trying to help the soldiers. They also claim that there is widespread looting in Beijing by bad elements.

∞∞∞∞∞∞∞∞

In the afternoon, hundreds of very angry Jilin Tech students marched off campus toward downtown. They carried banners covered with swastikas that said the Chinese government leaders were fascists and they chanted new slogans like "Li Peng, you will never live in peace."

---

[22] In 1989, Yang Shangkun was President of China and Vice Chairman and Secretary-General of the powerful Central Military Commission. He openly supported Zhao's position on the student movement at first, then switched his allegiance to Li's position. Yang's nephew, Yang Jianhua, commanded the 27th Group Army from Hebei, one of the primary units used on June 4th to attack Beijing

In the afternoon the BBC reported that the troops in Beijing are still firing on people and the death toll is rising.

∞∞∞∞∞∞∞∞∞

The Jilin Tech marchers returned to campus seven hours later. They said no one interfered with the march, but there were police in all the intersections and one teacher saw a truckload of soldiers go by. The fact that students could march through the city showed that the Jilin provincial government is not as dedicated to vicious repression as the national government.

The marchers say they shared the VOA/BBC news reports from Beijing with people on the street, but most of the people they talked to believe the government's story that the soldiers were fighting counterrevolutionaries. Some students said they were so upset that people believed the government's story that they cried all night.

The students told me that at one point during the march they sat down in the street at Xinfa Circle. After they were there a while, the Jilin Tech Communist Party Youth League Secretary came and threatened to call the police if the students didn't come back to campus. When people in the crowd around the students heard him threatening the students, they asked him who he was. When he told them he was the Youth League secretary, a few people in the crowd grabbed him and started to beat him up. The students said the crowd would probably have killed him but the students protected him. Someone said "Don't protect him, let us kill him. We'll knock him down and each one of us can step on him." The Youth League Secretary managed to escape without many injuries.

∞∞∞∞∞∞∞∞

After dinner, we saw people gathering in the Auto dorm commons so we went over to see what was going on. When we reached the commons we saw a crowd of angry, chanting students surrounding a burning effigy that had a swastika armband and a banner across its chest that said "Li Peng." There was a large funeral wreath of white flowers near the burning effigy.[23]

Democracy Wall had posters with news from the BBC and from students and their parents in Beijing. The posters say the death toll is estimated at two to three thousand people based on reports from the Beijing hospitals but there are rumors that soldiers are taking bodies from the hospitals to crematoriums so there can't be a complete count of casualties and victims can't be identified.

I got into a discussion with students about the truthfulness of news coverage in China and in the US. The students say that they don't believe what they hear on the CCTV news but they've gotten good at guessing the truth, which is usually the opposite of the CCTV report.

The students asked if I thought that the BBC and VOA news reports from Beijing were accurate. I told them that the reporting on the events in Beijing is probably as accurate as possible, but VOA and BBC may not always be accurate in their reporting about life in the US or England. They were surprised the US

---

[23] White is the color of mourning in China.

government does not control all the news sources in the US like the government does in China.

Someone told me that today the Northeast Teachers administration warned their students not to demonstrate or make speeches about the Democracy Movement or what's happening in Beijing. The administration said they would use any means necessary to stop them if they did.

Some students hope there will be a general strike in Beijing.

The VOA Chinese-language broadcast began and students crowded around two or three portable radios to listen. We left to get the kids ready for bed.

The nightly CCTV news showed a 15-second video of tanks driving down a Beijing street. There was no commentary with the video.

6/5 Monday

I walked to Classroom Building #1 for my 8 a.m. class. Since I was early, I went to the teachers' lounge where I found the English teachers listening to a tape of last night's Chinese-language VOA news report. The mood was very somber, very quiet. One minute before eight, someone I didn't know, probably an administrator, walked into the room, and told us to go to our classrooms. As we walked to our rooms, one of the teachers began playing a funeral march on his boom box. He was also wearing a white flower on his shirt.

The classrooms were all empty. A message on the blackboard in my classroom called on students to leave campus and spread the truth about the Democracy Movement all over the country.

As I walked out of my room, a teacher walked up to me and said "I guess that's it for the semester." I walked back to the teachers' lounge with him where the remaining teachers were listening to the rest of the VOA broadcast.

While the broadcast was playing I had a whispered conversation with the teacher next to me. He said everyone is sad about the loss of life in Beijing but they are also very angry with the government. He thinks the Chinese people will overthrow the government once they understand the government's extreme reaction to the student movement.

When the broadcast was over, I said goodbye to everyone, walked out of Classroom Building #1 for the last time and wandered over to Democracy Wall to get the latest news and rumors about the situation in Beijing.

I heard that last night at the Jilin Tech Democracy Movement meeting, the remaining students all agreed to leave the campus in the next two days.

One teacher said later that many people thought the Statue of Liberty was too radical, but they had tears in their eyes at the sight of the statue being bulldozed.

On a much more serious note, there is a rumor that troops are on the way to Changchun to enforce martial law and reopen all the universities.

Someone translated a poster for me with telephone reports from Beijing:
- o Four Jilin University students died on Tiananmen on June 4th.
- o Two tourists were wounded at the Beijing Hotel, a classy old hotel that's a few blocks from Tiananmen.

There was also a tragic story about four female students on Tiananmen who begged advancing soldiers not to hurt them. The soldiers bayoneted one of the women and shot the other three repeatedly. The story was told by a wounded student who lay perfectly still on the square for hours because anyone who moved was shot by the soldiers.

There are reports that resistance continues, and the number of wounded keeps growing.

∞∞∞∞∞∞∞∞

I got home in time to hear someone from the Waiban give us an official warning that they could only guarantee our safety if we are in the foreigners' compound or being escorted by one of their staff. They urged us not to leave the campus to watch demonstrations and not to take photographs. We said we understood.

Will Jilin Tech send us home so they don't have to be responsible for us in the midst of martial law or will they keep us here in the hope that the strike will end?

∞∞∞∞∞∞∞∞

Right after lunch we went to a memorial service in front of the Great Hall for the students killed yesterday. Hundreds of students wearing white armbands or white flowers stood quietly while a few students spoke and a funeral march was played. There was a lot of emotion, but no tears.

After the memorial service ended, we talked with students we knew. I heard a rumor that martial law would be instituted in Changchun at 6 p.m. tonight. Another person said the the infamous Yang Jia Jun would occupy the Jilin Tech, Northeast Teachers, and Jilin University campuses. Another student told me that there will be a student march today through Changchun but no Americans should go outside the school gates with the students.

The march formed up in front of the Great Hall soon after the memorial ceremony ended. A small group of students lined up in orderly rows behind some funeral wreaths and then marched away, headed for Stalin Boulevard. We did not go with them.

After we got back to the apartment, the Waiban called to say they were ready to take me to the Bank of China office on People's Circle. Since we'll be leaving China soon, we need to exchange the RMB we've saved for US dollars. [24] RMB can't be exchanged for another currency once you leave China, not even in Hong Kong where we will stop on the way back to the US. I'm going to do that exchange today.

I also hoped that a money order that my in-laws wired to us a few days ago would be waiting at the bank. We're probably going to leave Changchun more than a week earlier than we originally planned so we may need to change airline reservations or pay for an extended stay in a hotel if we get stuck somewhere. Sally's parents were kind enough to send us some extra cash that we might need to cover our exit expenses.

A little while after the march left campus, I rode off campus in the Waiban minivan with some other teachers and foreign students. The driver zigzagged around the neighborhood running his personal errands before he turned the van north and headed toward the bank. Activity on the side streets seemed normal but at some of the busier intersections there were small groups of people reading leaflets that the students had pasted onto walls.

When the van swung out onto Stalin Boulevard from a side street, I saw the Jilin Tech students' march about half a block behind us. The few dozen students, spread out over two of the Stalin Boulevard car lanes,

---

[24] Renminbi, the official Chinese currency

looked tiny and vulnerable compared to the powerful mass demonstrations of a just week ago. They marched resolutely forward, however, heads held high. I was really scared for them and in awe of their courage in marching into the unknown.

Our van quickly sped away from the students and reached People's Circle in a few minutes. I didn't see any other student marches and there were only a few police along the route we drove to the bank. There was normal activity on People's Circle.

We trooped into the Bank of China building and experienced a typical appointment at a Chinese institution—a long wait with a nice cup of tea followed by a burst of activity, then a disagreement, more waiting, and then more bursts of activity followed by final handshakes and goodbyes.

I returned to campus and joined Sally in separating our belongings into three piles—things we will carry back to the US, things we will mail to the US, and stuff we are going to leave behind. The leave-behind pile, located on the second floor landing, is a two-foot high pile of clothes, toys, and books.

After an hour or two of sorting, we walked to the nearby Friendship Department Store to buy two good quality suitcases.[25] The clerk said that other foreigners had been in the store lately buying suitcases. He assured us it was safe in Changchun and said we should stay.

Back on campus, I heard that earlier this week some auto workers used the Jilin University school radio

---

[25] The Friendship Store was the only store in town where you could buy quality foreign products.

station to broadcast a call for a strike at the auto factory, a strike that I don't think happened. Another person told me that Jilin University students marched to the auto factory today to talk to the workers about the Democracy Movement.

∞∞∞∞∞∞∞∞∞

Six p.m. came and went but we saw no troops or other signs of martial law on our campus.

∞∞∞∞∞∞∞∞∞

The newsreaders were only seen at the very beginning of tonight's 7 p.m. CCTV news. I heard a rumor today that some of the newsreaders have refused to read the prepared news scripts. We did see different newsreaders tonight but there's no way to know why the newsreaders were changed.

Most of the news broadcast was videotaped reports that might have been made anytime in the past week or two—stories about the arrests of scrap metal thieves, reports on important meetings, crop reports, etc.

Their report on yesterday's massacre was a 15-second video clip that showed tanks pulling into Tiananmen, bulldozers pushing down the "Goddess of Liberty," and soldiers cleaning the square. I wonder how they cleaned up the bloodstains.

∞∞∞∞∞∞∞∞∞

At 7:30, we saw the mayor of Changchun on TV. For a minute I thought it was the announcement of martial law in Changchun but he was only giving a report about a conference on cities that was going on in Changchun.

Tonight at 10:30 there was a short video segment showing damaged army vehicles and cars with bullet holes. There was no explanation of where, when, or why this happened.

∞∞∞∞∞∞∞∞

The government's version of the events on June 4, at least the version being show on CCTV, doesn't make sense. How did thousands of soldiers and hundreds of citizens get hurt if a small band of people is responsible for the trouble? Did an army of counterrevolutionaries somehow hide among the students and their supporters on Tiananmen Square? The attacks on people on the Beijing streets and on Tiananmen are never discussed in these reports, just the conspiracy. They're acting like the Democracy Movement never happened.

Who can put a stop to this insane attack on the students and the people of Beijing? Is there a person or a group of people in the Chinese government who can overrule Deng? Will someone in the army stand up for democracy and lead a coup? Someone has to do something!

∞∞∞∞∞∞∞∞

If the US takes strong action against China in retaliation for the army's brutal attack on the students, the Chinese government might launch an anti-American campaign. That could make it harder for us to get through customs when we leave the country or, in the worst case, cause them to detain and question us about what we've seen.

6/6 Tuesday

This morning VOA reported that PLA units are fighting other PLA units but it's not clear where this is happening. This is the first time we've heard about opposition within the army to the repression. Could the army overthrow the leaders of the repression? Since many influential army leaders like Yang Shangkun are involved in this repression, it's unlikely the army will rebel against the government.

We called Sally's parents in Minnesota to check in. They are very worried about us because the US media says the situation in China is dire. They want us to come home immediately.

Even through we're anxious about the situation in Beijing, it's quiet in Changchun so we think getting out of the country is more likely to expose us to danger than staying here for a while. On the other hand, the government's crackdown is only beginning and we could get caught up in the repression since we are on a campus where the student movement was very active. After some discussion, we decided it would be safer to leave soon than stay so we started discussing how to safely exit from China.

We have reservations for a June 14th flight from Beijing to Hong Kong and then reservations on a flight a day later from Hong Kong to the US. We could try to get an earlier flight from Beijing to Hong Kong but the Beijing airport is already crammed full of foreigners trying to leave the country. Even getting to the Beijing airport could be a problem since the main Beijing train station is closed and I don't know if the normal flights from Changchun to Beijing are operating.

Because of the potential problems getting into and out of the Beijing airport, we decided to find another way to get to Hong Kong where we can use the second leg of our plane tickets to the US.

We could fly from Changchun to Guangzhou in southern China. There are flights and trains to Hong Kong from there but we're not familiar with Guangzhou or the extent of the government crackdown there. If the situation is chaotic, we could get stuck there.

I would feel better about flying to Dalian where we can get a flight to Hong Kong. Dalian is an international port city in a neighboring province that we visited during the May Day holiday. Unfortunately, to get from Changchun to Dalian, we would have to first fly to Shenyang where I've heard there have been problems with roaming gangs in the last few days. I don't want to get stuck in Shenyang either, even if it has a US consulate.

We could take the train from Changchun to Dalian but I'm concerned about how vulnerable we would be on a train. VOA recently reported on a series of robberies and attacks on trains by "unruly elements." We'd be in the soft sleeper car, the most expensive ticket on the train, so we'd be the first target of looters or robbers.

∞∞∞∞∞∞∞∞∞∞

One of our fellow teachers reached the US Embassy in Beijing by phone after a number of attempts over several days but the person they talked to was not helpful. No, the US government is not going to sponsor evacuation flights from China to the US. No, the US government will not ask the airlines to add more flights from China to Hong Kong or to the US. No, they're not sure what the best route out of China is from Changchun. The embassy person did, however, seem interested in getting information from our friend about what's going on in Changchun right now.

∞∞∞∞∞∞∞∞∞∞

We heard a lot of rumors today.
- o Martial law will be enforced in Changchun soon and all foreigners in the city will be moved to our compound.
- o All domestic flights are about to be cancelled.
- o The Guomingtang, the dominant political party in Taiwan that the Communists drove out of China in the 1940s, are mobilizing their forces for an attack on China.
- o The Bank of China in Beijing is now closed.

I heard that today Jilin University students commandeered four city buses, parked them in a big intersection on Stalin Boulevard, set up loudspeakers on the buses, and broadcast the latest Chinese-language VOA and BBC news reports. They gave the busses back after the broadcasts were played.

∞∞∞∞∞∞∞∞∞∞

After a bit of debate in our family and some negotiations with the Waiban, we've decided to take the train to Dalian where we will get a flight to Hong Kong. Someone from the Waiban will escort us to

Dalian and pay for our hotel room and meals until we leave China.

We started our final packing. We're only planning to bring four pieces of luggage and four backpacks. Anything that we really want that can't get into the bags and backpacks is getting mailed home tomorrow. The "leave behind" pile in the upstairs hallway is getting quite large.

∞∞∞∞∞∞∞∞∞

There was a weird "news conference" on CCTV tonight. The presenters were a small group of Party leaders including Yuan Mu from the State Council and Zhang Gong, the martial law commander. They began by stating that China is in the middle of a serious counterrevolutionary plot. Instead of having reporters ask them questions about the situation, they took turns asking each other questions. Then the Beijing Party Chairman read a description of the events of the last few weeks in a monotone, shielding his eyes from the camera at one point. Their lies about this supposed counterrevolution are so incredible that they can't even look into the camera when they are repeating them! I'm scared for the Chinese people because these Party leaders will say or do anything to stay in power.

There were no onscreen newsreaders on the CCTV nightly news programs, only taped reports. The last time I saw the newsreaders on camera, they all wore black clothes. Have they all refused to participate in spreading the government's lies?

At 9 p.m. someone called and told us that thousands of autoworkers were marching north on Stalin Boulevard toward the provincial headquarters building. We rushed out to Stalin but we didn't see or hear a march.

Around 11 p.m., I heard the sound of a crowd singing—probably the echo of a demonstration somewhere on our side of town. Maybe it's the autoworkers.

At midnight I heard a loud rumbling that sounded like a long line of trucks driving down Stalin Boulevard. Is it the autoworkers or the Yang Jia Jun or something completely harmless? I won't find out until the morning.

6/7 Wednesday

I didn't sleep much last night. I was worrying about martial law and thinking about everything that could go wrong during our trip to Dalian.

At 5 a.m. the Changchun martial law proclamation was broadcast over the campus loudspeakers. The announcement said no one should spread rumors, participate in demonstrations, etc. I think we'll see troops in Changchun soon.

This morning VOA reported that the Communist Party installed the Public Security Chief as General Secretary of the Party. The security forces are now in charge of the country.

Later in the morning, I rode my bike downtown. Even though martial law has been declared, there's no sign of a crackdown here. There are no troops or police on the street and there still are Democracy Movement posters up on walls and funeral wreaths on People's Circle.

When I got back to campus, a student told me that 40-50,000 autoworkers rallied last night in front of the Geological Palace.

∞∞∞∞∞∞∞∞∞∞

Our Chinese friends ask when we'll come back to Changchun. We tell them that we don't know—it's an expensive and time-consuming trip and we have to get our careers started back in the US. They tell me that China is going to be okay, that this is a problem they will solve. They say it's just a matter of time until this government falls because the people intensely hate Deng Xiaoping, Li Peng, and their supporters and only their deaths will avenge the people's anger.

The Waiban thinks we should try to get on the CAAC flight from Dalian to Hong Kong in two days.[26] That means we need to leave Changchun by tomorrow night so we can make the flight. We'll take the evening train from Changchun to Dalian and hope it's an uneventful trip.

We got calls through to our parents in the US to update them on our plans. One call was cut off--I may have had said something a censor didn't like--but it may have been a normal phone system problem.

[26] The CAAC, Civil Aviation Administration of China, was China's government-controlled airline.

6/8 Thursday

The VOA morning broadcast reported that Chinese troops entered the US diplomatic compound in Beijing, technically an invasion of American territory. The army said they were chasing a sniper but it's probably just a show of force in retaliation for the US criticism of the crackdown on the students.

We went to a dorm to say goodbye to some friends and to give them some of our teaching materials. Our friends are still hopeful about China's future but they say they might have to fight for the China they want.

The Waiban called and said there was a mistake on our train tickets (I'm not sure who made the mistake) so our departure time to Dalian is moved from early evening to very late tonight. Our traveling party will include our family, two other teachers, and a Waiban staffer.

I really started worrying about the train trip. VOA recently reported that both roving outlaw gangs and groups of out-of-control soldiers have stopped and robbed trains in central China. We're in northeast China so maybe it's not a problem here but it's still a cause for concern.

One of our fellow teachers called the US consulate in Shenyang and told them about our plan to leave China through Dalian. The consulate said that as far as they knew our route is safe and we should advise them if we have any problems. I feel better after hearing them say the route is safe but I think the situation could change quickly.

We spent the rest of the day packing and talking with teachers, students, and Waiban staff who stopped by the apartment.

∞∞∞∞∞∞∞∞

CCTV is continuously broadcasting videos of June 4th and 5th in Beijing. Today I saw a new video that shows what looks like a group of average people blowing up an armored personnel carrier and attacking army trucks while a crowd of hundreds of onlookers cheer. Like the other propaganda videos, there is no information about where or when this was taped, who these people were, and what happened before people attacked the troops.

CCTV is also broadcasting videos that are aimed at promoting a positive view of the army. Today there was a video of smiling soldiers sweeping the streets in Beijing and helping appreciative old people do their chores.

∞∞∞∞∞∞∞∞

Tonight the Waiban held a small farewell banquet for all the departing teachers in the fancy dining room in the foreigner's compound. The banquet included some of our favorite dishes and the food was delicious.

A student invited to the banquet said a group of Jilin Tech students went to the Changchun Auto plant at 6 a.m. and used signs and a small bullhorn to urge the workers to strike in support of the Democracy Movement. The factory managers soon became aware of the students at the gate and used much larger speakers to tell workers to ignore the students. The student said the workers crossed the students' picket line, but the students plan to keep going to the plant to urge the younger autoworkers to strike while they talk to the more conservative older workers about the issues.

Unfortunately, the number of students available to do propaganda work at the plant is dwindling as students leave campus for home. The remaining students will get worn out since they have to get up at 5 a.m. and ride their bikes for fifty minutes to get to the plant before the first shift.

When the student finished telling us this story, a Waiban staffer asked, "Where did you hear that?" and the student replied, "I can't talk about that."

∞∞∞∞∞∞∞∞∞

By 9 p.m. all our stuff was packed and some Waiban staffers were looking through the leave-behind pile in the upstairs hallway.

∞∞∞∞∞∞∞∞∞

A handful of students and friends were there to say goodbye when we left for the train station at 10:54 p.m. Two women, probably from Hannah's kindergarten, gave Hannah and Mike good luck charms to wear and one of our favorite students gave me a lucky stone. The students are trying to be optimistic but they expect there to be a wave of repression against everyone associated with the student movement coupled with a major political campaign with an anti-Western edge.

122

We arrived at the mostly deserted Changchun train station a little after eleven and found out our train was running late. We sat for a while in the relatively comfortable foreigners' waiting room (there are sofas there instead of the hard benches in the regular waiting room), then moved to the train platform as the train's arrival time approached.

While we were waiting for our train, the Trans-Siberian Railway train (Moscow to Beijing) stopped on the same platform. Several passengers got off the train to smoke and our fellow teacher, who speaks Russian, went over to chat with them. These people had been on a train for six days and probably had no idea they were headed to a city where the army had brutally attacked civilians. They were very surprised to hear the news, but I don't think they had any option other than continuing to the end of their trip in Beijing.

Our train arrived in Changchun forty minutes late. It was after midnight by the time we were all settled in the soft sleeper car and the train left the station. The kids went right to sleep, but the Waiban staffer and I talked a bit about where I thought the trouble spots were going to be on the trip. I told him the most likely trouble spot was Shenyang, which we would reach about 4 a.m. that morning.

My exhaustion was more powerful than my fear and I fell asleep soon after the train left Changchun. Every time the train stopped at a station, I half woke up and leaned down from my upper bunk to peer out the window. I tried to decipher the characters for the station names but I was too groggy to keep track of our progress and luckily we ran into no problems.

6/9 Friday

At six-thirty this morning we were jolted awake by martial music blasting out of the speaker in the ceiling of the train car. The Chinese news broadcast that followed the music began with a warning to students that they must cooperate with the authorities in calming disorder.

The news also reported that "bad elements" in the cities of Chengdu and Lanzhou were looting stores and starting fires. I think criminals are taking advantage of the disorder since June 4th to loot and rob, and that really plays into the hands of a government that wants to portray the whole Democracy Movement as criminal.

We arrived at the Dalian train station about noon. A Waiban official from a Dalian university met us and took us to what we were told was a "safe" hotel. I think it's considered to be safe because it seems to be pretty far from downtown Dalian and any university campuses or neighborhoods.

∞∞∞∞∞∞∞∞∞

A group of faculty and students from Illinois State University in Normal, IL, was also at the hotel. On June 4th, this group was staying across the street from Beijing University, one of the centers of the Democracy Movement. The group members saw troops driving by on the street and moving around the Beijing University campus but they did not see or hear any fighting. Needless to say, they were shaken by the experience.

On June 5th the Illinois group got a very cool reception when they arrived in Dalian, which was the next stop on their tour of China. Only one faculty member came to their welcome banquet here and he just shook their hands and left. Also, the American professor leading the ISU delegation was told that his former Chinese students (he has taught at the Dalian university two different times) were not available to talk with him.

The rest of their tour is now cancelled and they are preparing to fly to Guangzhou and then out of China.

∞∞∞∞∞∞∞∞∞

In the late afternoon we went to the CAAC offices to buy plane tickets to Hong Kong. I expected to see lots of baggage-toting foreigners there, but there were only a few people in the ticket line. We couldn't get tickets on tomorrow's flight to Hong Kong but we did get reservations on a flight next Wednesday.

At least Dalian is a nice place to be stranded. Located on a long peninsula that juts out into the East China Sea, Dalian is China's third busiest port and largest export port so it's a very international city. Sure, it's polluted and crowded like other Chinese cities, but it has some interesting architecture, a beautiful location by the ocean, and delicious local cuisine that includes lots of very fresh seafood.

∞∞∞∞∞∞∞∞∞

The CCTV news tonight consisted of a number of very short video segments showing people building barricades, fighting troops, and firebombing trucks, followed by video showing smiling soldiers cleaning Beijing streets and helping old people. This is all designed to show, as the voiceover for the videotape said, that the counterrevolution is real and the soldiers are our friends.

A video segment, said to be from a surveillance camera on Tiananmen Square, showed a large group of students marching off the square at night. This is being shown to support the government's contention that students were allowed to leave Tiananmen unharmed on June 4th. But was this video really taken on June 4th and how many students were left on the square if this group did march off?

Next, there was video of Deng, Li, Yang Shangkun and the other military chiefs at a meeting, standing and applauding each other for their work of "suppressing counterrevolutionaries." I was really disgusted.

In their evening broadcast, VOA reported that the violence has stopped in Beijing. VOA also reported that Chinese authorities have arrested a number of student leaders and are searching in Beijing and other cities for student leaders that have avoided arrest.

VOA reported that large numbers of foreigners are leaving China.

Since the killing on the streets of Beijing seems to have stopped, the VOA reports on China are shorter and concentrate on the American response to the repression. Other than more news about Bush's pragmatic "wait and see" approach, which I still agree with, the political debate in the US about China isn't interesting to me. Those of us in China need hard news about what's going on here and we need to get it from foreign news sources!

6/10 Saturday

We moved to a hotel in downtown Dalian today. There will be more to see and do downtown and our Waiban person says the food in the new hotel's restaurant is very good.

The VOA morning news reported that Beijing is quiet and the government is hunting down fugitive student leaders. There also was a feature story about Americans evacuating from Wuhan.

We don't turn on the TV when we're in the hotel room because CCTV is now broadcasting the martial law authority videos continuously. This barrage of images has to influence the opinions of the hundreds of millions of Chinese who did not actually see the events in Beijing and have no alternative news sources.

Today, our fellow teachers talked with a teacher who decided to stay in Changchun. She reported that the Jilin Tech spring semester will officially end next week and the fall semester will start three weeks early to make up for the time lost this spring.

Today we heard that the Canadian government has chartered a plane that will take Canadians and Americans from Dalian to Tokyo tomorrow. We heard the flight is free but if we decide to go on that charter we will forfeit the $700 we paid for nonrefundable CAAC tickets to Hong Kong. Also, going to Tokyo would mean expensive hotel rooms and expensive new flight arrangements from Tokyo to the US. That doesn't seem like a good idea.

The CCTV nightly news featured video of people that were arrested for causing disorder. These people looked like the unsavory "dregs of society," that the government says are one of the causes of the current disorder. I don't think it would be very popular to show arrested student leaders on the news because the Chinese love the university students and see them as the future of the country.

There was also video of injured soldiers being visited in a hospital by Communist Party leaders. Where are the pictures of the thousands of Beijing citizens who were killed or injured by the army!? Not on CCTV news.

6/11 Sunday

This morning VOA reported that most of the Americans who want to leave China have left. I'm skeptical—I don't think the US government has any idea how many Americans were in China before June 4th, how many Americans are in China are now, and how many of them want to leave.

We have decided not to pursue the free Canadian flight to Tokyo.

Are we in danger here? Things seem very quiet in Dalian, but will US-China relations sour quickly and put Americans in China in danger? Bush seems to be solid on his pragmatic approach toward China but will Congress override him?

∞∞∞∞∞∞∞∞∞∞

This afternoon, CCTV broadcast a new series of videos from June 4th. First, there was the video of students marching off Tiananmen Square, then a few minutes of video showing the army tearing down and burning banners, tents, and signs on Tiananmen. Next, there was a short segment showing soldiers sweeping and tidying up the Square. The last segment showed Beijing residents happily talking with the soldiers.

Where is the video of soldiers shooting their way through Beijing? How many students remained on Tiananmen when some students marched off and where's the video of what happened between the time the students marched off Tiananmen and the soldiers began the cleanup there? Did the government destroy that video?

After those videos, they showed a news reporter asking a small group of people on a campus what they thought about the rumors of mass arrests. The people he questioned said they didn't know anything about mass arrests, but they said they had heard the police arrested some guys for stealing some tapes, a Newsweek, and some souvenir buttons. The announcer added that police also picked up a few students who were involved in some kind of trouble with an illegal business. That proves there were no mass arrests!

∞∞∞∞∞∞∞∞∞∞

We found out that the Canadian charter flight is to Hong Kong and it isn't free. You have to sign a pledge to pay if you can't pay on the spot. Also, they aren't reserving seats, just telling people to show up at the airport.

If we decide to give up our CAAC tickets and take the Canadian flight but we can't get on the Canadian flight because it's full, we could get stuck here for three or four more days until the next CAAC flight to Hong Kong. Will the Waiban get sick of paying our hotel and food bills if that happens? Tomorrow we're going to ask CAAC again about their refund policy.

The BBC afternoon broadcast reported that the government held a rally in Changchun to denounce the student leaders of the Changchun Democracy Movement. There were no details. Did they denounce people we knew? We'll wait for the CCTV news tonight to see if they report on the rally.

∞∞∞∞∞∞∞∞∞

The CCTV nightly news tonight was almost ninety minutes long instead of the usual sixty minutes. The overall message was that everything is back to normal, the soldiers are your friends, and there were no massacres.

The broadcast started with video from Beijing of soldiers cleaning streets, sleeping on the hard stone of Tiananmen, helping people clean windows, and visiting schools.

Next, one of the announcers denounced people that spread the rumor that a massacre happened in Beijing on June 4th. He told the story of a man who spread the rumor that thousands of students were beaten on June 4th. This man was arrested today for spreading rumors (we saw video of him in handcuffs) and now he admits he couldn't have seen everything he said he did. He apparently does still say he saw some beatings.

Next, they showed an interview with a pair of women who said that some guy had told them that soldiers beat an old man and a seven-year-old. The women asked, "How could that have happened?" Then the news announcers read letters from CCTV viewers that objected to VOA's rumormongering and urged the Chinese to listen to Chinese news, not American news.

When the official Chinese press attacks foreign media, they always go after VOA, although they do sometimes attack the BBC. I'm not sure why they go easier on the BBC since both news services provided in-depth coverage of the student movement that was sympathetic to the students and very critical of the government.

There was no news about the rally in Changchun.

∞∞∞∞∞∞∞∞

I have no doubt that the propaganda barrage on CCTV is convincing people all over China that the government's version of what happened on June 4th is true. The government's complete control of the media has allowed them to rewrite the events of the last few months and turn attention away from the pro-Democracy demands of the largest popular movement in China in decades.

It really looks like the Democracy Movement is completely crushed. I'm afraid that all the leaders of the movement plus prominent movement supporters from all walks of life will be rounded up and sent to prison if they don't escape to the West. The next time a people's movement starts to develop, the government will probably smash it immediately.

6/12 Monday

Our four backpacks and four suitcases were packed and ready to go right after breakfast, just in case we left Dalian today on the Canadian flight.

At breakfast, our friends told us they had called the remaining American teacher in Changchun and she had nothing to report because no teachers or students had come to visit her the day before. One Chinese teacher told her two days ago that she wouldn't visit her anymore. Everyone is preparing for the crackdown ahead and I'm sure no one wants to be seen spending time with foreigners.

VOA reports that Democracy Wall advocates from 1979 are being arrested and arrest warrants were issued for Fang Lizhi and his wife, who are currently safe in the US embassy in Beijing. [27] The warrant for Fang Lizhi could lead to a direct confrontation between Chinese and US soldiers at the US embassy gates.

After breakfast we walked to the CAAC office where Sally asked how much of a refund we could get on the tickets. They say they will give us 75% back if we cancel the reservation.

---

[27] Fang Lizhi was an influential physicist and outspoken critic of the Chinese government's policies on education and human rights. Fang and his wife Li Shuxian had talked about Chinese politics with some of the Democracy Movement's leaders.

We went outside the CAAC office and discussed the pros and cons of getting a refund and leaving today on the Canadian charter flight. We're safe here and well looked after by the Waiban but our family is crowded into a small hotel room with two narrow beds and we're bored because we haven't found a lot to do in Dalian.

We decided to try to get on the charter flight. We're going to leave today!

We got the partial refunds for the CAAC tickets, and then hurried to the hotel where the kids and I, with some help from our fellow teachers, brought our bags to the lobby. Meanwhile, Sally went to the Bank of China to change our last RMB to dollars. The Waiban staffer got us a taxi and the staffer, the kids, and I crowded in. We picked up Sally at the bank and we were off to the Dalian airport!

We got to the airport at noon. The Waiban staffer collected our resident alien ID cards and left immediately in the same cab, saying he had an appointment. Just a quick handshake and he was gone.

Outside the terminal building I was stopped by a film crew who said they were Canadians working for ABC News. They asked me some questions about my experiences during the last week, and then asked me if they could film me answering the same questions. I did answer the questions on film but my answers were pretty vague since I didn't want to say anything that might get someone in trouble.

Inside the terminal building we met a US consular official from Shenyang—the first US Foreign Service staffer we had seen in China. She asked us about the size of the student movement in Changchun, about our trip to Dalian, and why we decided to take the flight today. She said the consular staff thinks that Changchun had more Democracy Movement activity than the huge city of Shenyang where the consulate is located.

She told us the Alberta provincial government chartered a Dragon Air 737 for today's flight to bring thirty-five Canadian students out of China but other foreigners were welcome on the plane. The Canadians will get tickets first and board first.

Our family waited fairly patiently for at least an hour in the terminal building for some news about the flight. During that hour the handful of foreigners waiting in the terminal for the flight slowly became a small crowd.

At about 1:00 p.m., everyone waiting for the Canadian flight was told to move to the nearby International Terminal. When the plane landed forty minutes later, they issued us tickets and we lined up in front of a table in the customs area. At this point, I thought there were about thirty people from the US and other countries waiting for the flight along with the Canadians.

Unfortunately, there were no customs officials waiting to process our exit from China. We waited in line for an hour before a small group of uniformed customs police marched into the building. Two of the grim-faced customs officers sat down at the table and set up their stamps and forms while another customs officer, who seemed to be in charge, positioned himself near the table where he could watch over the process. The standing customs officer was soon flanked by a Canadian consular official and the American consular official.

I watched people being questioned by the customs officers as we slowly moved toward the front of the line. The police seemed to be carefully reading and conferring about each person's passport and visa. By the time it was our turn at the Customs table, three or four people had been asked to wait beside the table, presumably for further discussion with the customs officials.

We rolled up to the Customs table with two luggage carts, a child sitting on top of each one. I don't think we intentionally put the kids up there to charm the Customs police (the Chinese really love kids!), but all three custom officials broke into big smiles when they saw the kids.

We emphasized that we were teachers, teachers being the least suspicious foreigners. They asked us for the resident alien cards that our Waiban staffer had collected and then taken with him when he left the airport. The customs police thought they should have collected the cards but after a short conference with the customs officer in charge, they said it was okay.

They stamped our passports and we moved to baggage inspection where we had to have a short discussion with the officer about an American boombox we left with friends in Changchun. After a few minutes they said it was okay, stamped our paperwork, x-rayed our luggage, checked our persons, gave us boarding passes, and sent us through to something they called "quarantine" where someone else checked our passports. We ended up in another waiting area with the other passengers who had cleared customs.

It was now 5 p.m. and we were tired, hungry, and thirsty, and though officially across the Chinese frontier, we were still solidly on Chinese soil. A passenger who gave us a bag of cookies for the kids said she thought it would be another one or two hours before we left.

But only thirty minutes later it was time to board!! Everyone jumped up and headed for the exit. The crowd was high-spirited as we walked out the door, across the pavement, up a set of metal stairs and into the airplane.

When the plane left the ground there was a burst of applause from the passengers. When we reached cruising altitude, people got up and wandered around, probably trading stories about where they were on June 4th. I got up to stretch my legs and saw a group gathered around a copy of Time magazine with "Massacre" on the cover. I wanted to see a news report about June 4th from outside of China but I was too tired to join the group of strangers. The four of us just ate the meal they served and rested.

The night landing at Hong Kong was incredible. During an approach to Kowloon airport, planes fly in-between the dozens of brightly lit high-rise apartment buildings. When the plane touched down there was another burst of applause from the passengers.

At the baggage claim a man approached me and asked if I had just come out of China. He said he was from the US consulate in Hong Kong and was collecting the names of Americans to update their list of Americans that have left China. [Note: Later that day the US government China Crisis hotline reported to my mother that Sally and I left China but Michael and Hannah did not!]

After we claimed our bags at the airport, everyone on the flight was guided onto chartered buses that took us to the Hong Kong YMCA, a nice downtown hotel where the Alberta government had reserved rooms for all of us for three days at a greatly discounted rate. In another hour we were safe and comfortable in our beautiful hotel room (which unfortunately only had two single beds).

Epilogue 1: 6/13-6/15

Hong Kong is a very beautiful city with lots of cool places to visit, but our immediate goal was to quickly get on a plane to the US. The morning after we arrived, Sally took the train to the airport to try to get seats on a flight home in the next few days. Northwest Airlines told her there were no open seats until next week unless we wanted to pay several thousand more dollars to buy business class tickets, something we couldn't afford to do. Northwest also refused to transfer our tickets to another airline that had open seats on a flight the next day. Fortunately, later that day a travel agent we contacted got us a flight out of Hong Kong in just two days.

I was very mad at the airlines. Throughout this crisis, they just ran their regular flight schedules even though there were thousands of people stranded in China and Hong Kong. On our first day in Hong Kong, we called the US consulate to appeal for help with Northwest and they told us that we should call some relatives and have them send us the money to buy the Business Class seats. Thanks a lot.

Hong Kong was full of fleeing teachers and diplomatic families, all with some kind of news or rumor about what was going on in China. The wife of an embassy secretary reassured us that the Fan Lizhi situation was not as serious as it seemed because there was still communication between Chinese and American diplomats in Beijing. She also told us the army shot the CCTV newsreader who did the dramatic protest on the news broadcast the day of the

140

military   commands   statement   about   clearing
Tiananmen Square.

Another teacher from Changchun heard that police
took away truckloads of Changchun students and
workers at the end of last week. A teacher from Jinan
also reported arrests in her city. There was no way to
confirm any of these reports.

One of my most exciting experiences was turning on
the TV in the hotel room and seeing a CNN news
broadcast in English. The coverage centered on the
response in Hong Kong to June 4th with little talk
about exactly what happened in Beijing.

On June 15th we finally boarded a flight to LA,
arrived one hour later on the clock, and then two
hours   later   took   a   flight   from   LA   to
Minneapolis. Family members met us at the airport
and friends and neighbors (and our dog) greeted us at
our   house.   We   were   very   happy   to   be   home.

Epilogue 2: Twenty-five Years Later

By the time we returned to the US, the events of June 4th were already out of the US media headlines so, in those pre-internet days, we had a hard time finding news about the situation in China. We did get some news from other English teachers who had maintained connections with people in China but we never found out if anyone in Changchun was punished for their participation in the Democracy Movement.

Over the next four or five years we traded letters with some of our former students. Most of them graduated and accepted the jobs assigned to them but one student went to Shenzhen after graduation and built a career in the wild world of a free economic zone. None of them offered any information about the aftermath of the Democracy Movement and we didn't ask about it.

A few of our Changchun friends came to the US to attend graduate school and stayed after they graduated. We don't talk about the Democracy Movement with them either.

∞∞∞∞∞∞∞∞∞∞

Everyone in the family except me has visited China since 1989, although Michael is the only one who has visited Changchun. Michael reported that Jilin Tech is now part of Jilin University and many of the Jilin Tech campus buildings have been torn down and replaced, but the foreigners' compound, Classroom

142

Building #1, and his primary school were unchanged. He even talked with some of his primary school teachers.

∞∞∞∞∞∞∞∞∞

The problems identified by the Democracy Movement--growing income inequality, the collapse of the rural economy, and official corruption--have grown much worse since 1989.

According to reports in Beijing News, the GINI coefficient (a widely used measure of economic equality where 0.0 is perfect income equality and 1.0 is complete inequality) went from 0.275 in the 1980s to 0.438 at the end of 2010, higher than the UN's "warning point" of 0.4.[28] (In comparison, many estimates put the GINI coefficient for the US at between .42 and .47.) The World Bank, in a report published in February 2014, stated "the sustained increase in income inequality places China at the high end of income inequality among Asian countries."

The economic situation in the countryside is now so bad that over 260 million rural Chinese have been forced to move to cities to find work to support their families.[29] These migrant workers usually are not

---

[28] "China faces instability risks as gap between rich, poor widens," http://articles.economictimes.indiatimes.com/2012-09-17/news/33902854_1_gini-coefficient-inequality-economic-reforms; "Income inequality on the rise in China" http://www.aljazeera.com/indepth/features/2012/12/2012122311167503363.html

[29] "China Now Has More Than 260 Million Migrant Workers Whose Average Monthly Salary Is 2,290 yuan ($374.09)," http://www.ibtimes.com/china-now-has-more-260-million-migrant-workers-whose-average-monthly-salary-2290-yuan-37409-1281559

entitled to national healthcare, a pension, or free education for their children in the cities where they work since their household registration is in the countryside although the size of the migrant population is forcing reforms in this policy.[30] For this reason, a large number of children now remain in the countryside to go to school and be raised by relatives, often only seeing their parents during the New Years holidays.[31]

The official corruption denounced by the Democracy Movement in 1989 is pervasive today and the value of that influence has increased. People like Jiang Zemin's son, Jian Mianheng, have cashed in on their family's position to make vast fortunes. The New York Times states that "over the past two decades, business and politics have become so tightly intertwined, they say, that the Communist Party has effectively institutionalized an entire ecosystem of crony capitalism."[32] In a 2011 report, the People's Bank of China stated that 17,000 Communist Party members and state functionaries had illegally obtained and smuggled as much as $124 billion out of China from the mid-1990s until 2008.[33]

---

[30] "China struggles with growing urbanization," http://www.aljazeera.com/indepth/features/2012/12/20121223 142623649526.html; "China's Hukou Reform Plan Starts to Take Shape",http://blogs.wsj.com/chinarealtime/2014/08/04/chinas-houkou-reform-plan-starts-to-take-shap/.

[31] "Millions of Chinese rural migrants denied education for their children," http://www.theguardian.com/world/2010/mar/15/china-migrant-workers-children-education

[32] "Princelings" in China Use Family Ties to Gain Riches" http://www.nytimes.com/2012/05/18/world/asia/china-princelings-using-family-ties-to-gain-riches.html?_r=0

[33] "In China, Corruption and Unrest Threaten Autocratic Rule, The Atlantic," http://www.theatlantic.com/international/archive/2011

ᴏᴏᴏᴏᴏᴏᴏᴏᴏᴏᴏ

The violent suppression of the Democracy Movement and the ongoing intimidation of dissidents in China have not stopped the Chinese from fighting for their rights. In an article for the *Economic Observer*, Sun Liping, a professor at Tsinghua University, cites research estimating that there were 180,000 protests, riots and other mass incidents in China in 2010.[34] China Labour Bulletin, a Hong Kong group that monitors the labor situation in China and advocates for collective bargaining, documented 1039 strikes for better wages or to collect wage arrears in 2013.[35] Besides battles over economic issues, there are frequent reports of rioting connected to government land foreclosures and high levels of toxic pollution from manufacturing.[36] People also demanded changes after government corruption was connected to schools collapses during the Szechuan earthquake and to train crashes on the poorly engineered national high-speed rail system.[37]

/06/in-china-corruption-and-unrest-threaten-autocratic-rule/241128/

[34] "China's Challenge: Social Disorder, Economic Observer," http://www.eeo.com.cn/ens/feature/2011/05/09/200868.shtml

[35] "China Labour Bulletin Strike Map," http://www.numble.com/PHP/mysql/clbmape.html

[36] Farmers in China's South Riot Over Seizure of Land. http://www.nytimes.com/2011/09/24/world/asia/land-dispute-stirs-riots-in-southern-china.html?_r=0; "Kunming pollution protest is tip of rising Chinese environmentalism," http://www.theguardian.com/environment/chinas-choice/2013/may/16/kunming-pollution-protest-chinese-environmental-activism

[37] "China Admits Building Flaws in Quake," The New York Times, http://www.nytimes.com/2008/09/05/world/asia/05china.html?

∞∞∞∞∞∞∞∞∞

How many people died on the streets of Beijing and on Tiananmen on June 4-5, 1989? What happened to those missing since then? Only the Chinese government knows the whole truth.

The truth won't stay hidden forever. I believe there will be a full accounting of the events of June 3-4, 1989.

∞∞∞∞∞∞∞∞∞

The three weeks from mid-May to early June in 1989 were an extraordinary time for me, full of exhilaration, anxiety, sorrow and a tiny bit of fear. I'm still amazed that I had the opportunity to march alongside the participants in one of the largest political movements in Chinese history and to witness their commitment to the fight for democracy even when it was clear it could threaten their careers and possibly their lives. I hope this journal helps others understand the courage it took for them to make that commitment.

_r=0; "Boss Rail," The New Yorker, http://www.newyorker.com/reporting/2012/10/22/121022fa_fact_osnos?currentPage=all

Acknowledgements

I could not have completed this project without a lot of help. Thanks to my children, Michael and Hannah, for reading several versions of the journal and providing important input and encouragement. Thanks to my spouse Sally for providing her notes, her translations, and her comments on the journal. Thanks to Amy Smith who created the beautiful map of Changchun, to Marylee Hendricks and Kay Hanson who provided edits of drafts, and to Judy Krauss for reading a draft and providing input.

Appendix. A Snapshot of My Students' Attitudes

In the spring of 1989, before the Democracy Movement swept the campus, I gave my students a questionnaire to capture their attitudes toward their futures, their country, and the US.

(Note: Not everyone answered every question and the student's spelling was maintained.)

Every bulleted item represents one answer. If the answer was given more than once, the number of times that answer was given is in parentheses next to the answer.

1. When you get your first job, what will be most important?

- o   Earning a lot of money – (4)
- o   Doing work that helps develop China (8)
- o   Both

How many yuan would you like to earn every month when you start working? [The exchange rate at the time was 8 yuan per US dollar.]

- o   200 – 5
- o   300 - 3
- o   400
- o   500
- o   1,000

o 10,000
o As many as possible
o I don't know

2. Do you want to study abroad?

Yes – 13
No -- 0

In what country?
o US (12),
o Australia
o Russia
o Japan

3. If you had to choose one country in the world to live in other than China, what country would you choose?

o Swiss (3)
o US (3)
o Germany (5)
o France
o Singapore
o China

4. If you had 100,000 yuan, what would you do?

What would you buy?

o Color TVs and recorder
o Computer and electronics lab equipment
o A factory with modern machines
o I would study abroad
o A car (3)
o I would buy a mass of land and grow

fruit trees there, eat the fruit and play in the woods everyday
- I would travel around the world
- I'll buy a lot of good foods.
- I'd like to use on business and get more money. If I have time to do business I could lend it to others and take advantage from them.
- I will go abroad to study, perhaps to the US to meet my brother-in-law and learn drills which is useful to my future. If left, I will travel around world, first Swiss or Germany, Austrailia, Hawaii island, etc.
- I would build a study for me.
- I'll invest half of it to my business.
- I'll buy a house in the big city for my parents
- Buy books and furniture
- Education (2)

How much would you save?

- 10,000 and invest the rest
- 10,000 (2)
- 2,000 yuan (3)
- One third of it
- Not even a little
- I would save nothing (2)
- All

Would you give money away?

- Some money to my parents
- No (3)
- If possible (2)
- If someone really needed money, I would give him some.

- I want the teachers in our university share with the funds to improve their living conditions to some degrees

5. Write two or three words that describe America (For example, big, dirty, crazy)

- Prosperous (2)
- Powerful (2)
- Advanced (2)
- Hard work
- Travel
- Developed (5)
- Free (2)
- Busy (2)
- Dangerous (1)
- Crazy (2)
- Ill
- Cruel
- Mixture
- Civilized
- Pretensive
- Competitive (2)
- Strong
- Noisy
- Rich (2)
- Warm hearted
- Pride
- Great
- Terrible
- Temptation

6. Write two or three words that describe China.

- Poor (4)
- Powerful

- o Great (2)
- o Crowded
- o Too many people
- o Developing (9)
- o Traditional
- o Out of control
- o Old (3)
- o Old Fashioned
- o Big (4)
- o Too wise to develop
- o Beautiful (2)
- o Hopeful (2)
- o Stale
- o Unefficient
- o Large
- o Kind
- o Strong
- o Lively
- o Warmhearted

7. Many people see the US as an imperialist power, using its military forces to force other countries to do what the US wants. Do you agree?

Yes (12)
No (2)

Why or why not?
- o Because US invade a lot of countries, force them to yield
- o It made a competition of weapons with the USSR and breaks the peace of the whole world, also the event of Taiwan
- o Because the US has already forced other countries to do what the US wants. For example, the countries in Latin America.

- o Americans want to be free but does anybody think it's right to get freedom which is based on other people's chains?
- o Some countries had to do what the US told them because they were afraid of the military forces.
- o I don't know what the brass talks of it's freedom
- o To some degree military forces is an indication of a country. Most of the imperialist powers can do this, it is the fact which is understandable
- o Because of the existence of United Nations, US can't clearly to threaten the others but I think US has the hope to control the others, now pay more attention on economic.
- o Because big country always keep it's leadership in the world. Want to be more superior of my other one. Want to become more big and most rich.
- o Such is fact
- o Because of Taiwan

8. Do you think the election of George Bush will lead to a better relationship between the US and China?

> Yes (12)
> No (1)

Why or why not?
- o I think George Bush likes China
- o He is an old friend of China
- o The world situation forces his to do so and he has more touch with China and knows more about China
- o For several months he promises without action

- o Because as soon as he became president he visited China. This means he attached much importance to make a better relationship between China and US
- o Because he visited China after he had just been elected, it showed that he wanted to improve the relationship between two countries.
- o I don't know. Let history tell the truth.
- o In the history, he was a friend of China and also he declared he would be like that. I think he should be better to China.
- o George Bush is good at business he know, China is a big fellow on trade and also a big marker. He can get a lot from China.
- o Reagan like Taiwan much. Bush likes education look like the knowledge up. He may be wise an honest. Also cause he worked in China once.
- o Because he have worked in China some year ago
- o He is kind enough

9. Do you think trade between the US and China will grow in the next ten years?
    - o Yes (13)
    - o No

    Will it grow quickly or slowly?
    - o Quickly (6)
    - o Slowly (6)

10. What is the most important thing China can learn/import from the US?

- o The basion industry
- o Science and technology (2)
- o Modern machines
- o Full of creative and risky spirit
- o Attach great importance to education
- o Different parties discussed everything together
- o Rich policy for country
- o Control the economic system by a valid hand.
- o Pay more attention on technique. Develop the economic, not only struggle for the politics
- o Very developed technology of science, industry, management and attitude to education. Especially the last one.
- o Technique
- o Freedom (2)
- o Philosophy
- o Power is economic

11. What is the most important thing the US can learn/import from the China?

- o Respecting the old
- o China welcomes American to China on business
- o Traditional culture
- o College students (in the future they're doctors)
- o This question should be replied by an American
- o Everything
- o Care for people's life conditions
- o Respect old people
- o Pay more attention to the political society, don't get a havoc which destroy the nation.

- o Support the weak, country, low rate of crime and divorce
- o Treating people honestly, supporting the weak countries
- o Peaceful
- o Realism
- o Friendship among Chinese

12. What country do you think is China's best friend in the world today?

- o Japan (4)
- o W. Germany
- o No Country (4)
- o North Korea
- o No one (2)

What country will be China's best friend in ten years?

- o US(2)
- o Russia (2)
- o Germany
- o No Country (3)
- o I don't know (3)

13. Is it important for China to have a good relationship with the Soviet Union?
Yes (12)
No

Why or why not?
- o Because the Soviet Union is strong and has a lot of army
- o The two countries need each other
- o Good relationships should be kept between powers
- o Because Soviets border on China. Two

countries have a very long border and same social system

o Both China and the Soviet Union will get a benefit if they have a good relationship

o Soviet Union is a power country. If China have a good relationship.

o We are neighbors and it should be easy to get a coordination for each other. We all have some scarcity that can be rescued by each other.

o Soviet Union is the biggest neighbor of China. The two countries know each other well. Friendship between the countries' people keep good.

o Because Soviet Union is strong enough to conquer our country

o Developed vs. economic

o Improve our influence

o Defend the world war

o Our neighbor

14. Many people in the US are afraid that a nuclear war will destroy the world.

Do you think a nuclear war could happen?
o Yes, it's possible (6)
o No, it's not possible (5)

Do you think a nuclear war will happen?
o Yes (4)
o No (8)

15. How long do you think it will take China to solve it's economic problems, problems like inflation and uneven development?
o 100 years (2)
o 70 years
o 50 yrs. (2)

   o 30 yrs (2)
   o 20 yrs (3)
   o Many

16. What do you think is the worst problem in China today? (Problems include inflation, problems in education, shortages, differences in wealth between East and West, corruption)

   o Corruption (3)
   o Problems in education (6)
   o Illness in mind
   o Management systems
   o Population
   o Shortages
   o Prices

17. Many in the West say that China is becoming a capitalist country. Do you think this is true?

Yes (4)
No (6)

Why or why not?
   o China is poor and has a lot of people instead of a lot of money
   o Chinese people are great but it'll take a long time and hard work to be the capitalists.
   o China only learns some good point from western and some bad things also come into accompany our learning. In fact, China is not becoming a capitalist country.
   o Are you crazy? We are friendly to you foreigners. We will introduce you to a good doctor.

- o China has a large population, it become powered than before
- o We can cover society government but we can't cover productive power. We have to add something which is popular in capitalist country to our production or creation to service the people.
- o Because Chinese people have a good cultural tradition and honest spirit. For example. Supposedly North Korea in 1952.
- o Chinese is clever and work hard.